CW00523987

HOW TO WRITE SCIENCE FICTION

HOW TO WRITE SCIENCE FICTION

Bob Shaw

a&b

First published in Great Britain in 1993 by
Allison & Busby
an imprint of Wilson & Day Ltd
5 The Lodge
Richmond Way
London W12 8LW

A catalogue record for this title is available from the British
Library

ISBN 0 74900 135 6

Phototypeset by Intype, London
Printed and bound in Great Britain by
Mackays of Chatham PLC, Chatham, Kent

For Mike and Debby
who are always ready to help.

CONTENTS

INTRODUCTION

This book is specifically about how to write science fiction.

For that reason, it does not contain much on the general theory of writing – information which can be gleaned at writing classes or from numerous books. Instead, I have concentrated on putting into no-nonsense language the most useful things I have learned in almost forty years of writing and selling science fiction. This is a how-to-do-it book in the truest sense. Hard-won trade secrets are revealed on practically every page, so if you can't write successful science fiction after reading it – you have only yourself to blame!

One point about grammar. At school I was taught one of Doctor Johnson's major precepts – where necessary or convenient, the male form of a word stands for both male and female. I was about seven at the time and already was aware of some problems in the construction of neat, lean sentences where I had to keep saying 'he or she' and 'his or her'. When my teacher handed on the good doctor's advice, I clearly remember thinking, 'What a sensible idea! This is going to make writing so much simpler.'

I swear to you that if the teacher had said the *female* form of a pronoun was to be preferred, I would have just as happily gone along with it. Throughout this book, therefore, 'his' can mean 'his or hers', and 'he' can mean 'he or she'. I am not involved in some anti-feminist conspiracy. (A bonus for all of us is that I have not had to use the overlong and convoluted constructions to which some modern writers resort in order to avoid dealing with gender.)

Fifty years ago women were virtually unknown in the science-fiction community – as writers, readers, editors or agents – but the current situation is vastly different, and the entire scene has benefited as a result.

Enough shilly-shallying, as Groucho Marx would have said; let's get on with the business of discovering how to write science fiction. I say 'discovering' because the mere act of putting down on the page what I have learned in almost forty years – during which I sold *every word that I wrote* – has crystallised many things in my mind. Having written it, perhaps *I* will become a better science-fiction writer.

This is not a huge book but it is densely packed with straight information, so I would suggest that firstly you read it straight through and get the general feel of what it's all about, then refer back to passages of particular interest. As I say at the very end, writing science fiction is almost a science-fiction adventure in itself.

So, go to it! Enjoy every hour of your personal journey, and – if you make a lot of money on the way – think about buying me a pint some time . . .

1

STARTING A SUCCESSFUL CAREER

This is a book about how to write science fiction – so let's get one thing clear from the start.

I have earned my living solely by the pen since 1960, and regard myself as a dedicated writer with an abiding love for the art. But when I talk about 'writing' herein the word has a wider meaning than the various techniques of filling pages with satisfactory prose. Throughout this book 'writing' will always mean 'writing and getting published and receiving money for one's hard work'.

There are lots of people who treat writing as a semi-private pursuit. They see it as a pleasant way of passing a few hours and have little interest in plunging into the hurly-burly of the marketplace. That is a legitimate approach – and there is no reason such people shouldn't find the following pages of interest – but to me writing is part of the concept of communication. When I write something I want it to be read by as many people as possible, and that means going into print. A consequence of getting published is that you receive money, and the general rule is that the larger your audience the bigger the cheques. The more money you bring in, the better placed you will be to carry on writing. It's a case of Mammon and the Muses walking hand in hand . . .

The above possibly goes without saying, but I have no

time for the notion that private writing is somehow 'finer' than published matter. You should enjoy writing, but while you're at the desk it does no harm to remember that you would also enjoy things like seeing your name in book and magazine shops and libraries, becoming a celebrity locally if not worldwide, having author's copies to give to your friends (and enemies), signing autographs, being interviewed by the press, receiving royalties, etc.

In case I'm giving the impression that this is a manual on how to become a commercial hack, I must mention a vital principle which has kept me going through 25 novels and 80 published short stories. To make money from writing you have to write for the market – especially in science fiction – but the wonderful truth is that you do not have to surrender your creative individuality. Writing to please yourself is not necessarily incompatible with writing to please the public. You *can* say what you want to say. The best published writing often comes from people who have mastered all the marketing skills and at the same time have learned to stamp their work with their own personality, and to infuse it with their own uniqueness.

Yes, you can have your literary cake and eat it. The trick is to observe the commercial rules but to regard them as an extra challenge, one you will actually *enjoy* meeting and which will bring out the very best in your own committed, heartfelt writing.

Having touched on some general precepts which apply to all branches of writing, let's get down to particulars which apply only to science fiction . . .

What is science fiction?

It may surprise a newcomer to sf to learn that the above question has been perplexing old hands in the field for many years. Nobody has been able to come up with a succinct yet comprehensive definition. By comparison, it is easy to define the Western, the historical romance, the detective story, and so on. Science fiction has a strange and somewhat infuriating ability to transcend the usual publishers' categories.

It isn't enough to say that it consists of stories about the future – although sf usually has a futuristic setting, it can quite easily be set in the present, the past, or in a time frame which has nothing to do with Earthly calendars. You can't even get away with saying that it involves stories in which scientists and their activities play an important part. Some perfectly good mainstream novels (such as Neville Shute's *No Highway*) fit that description but are not classed as sf because they lack the genre's unique element.

On the other hand, many stories which undoubtedly *are* good sf have no discernible connection with scientists or science, but they fit comfortably into the classification because they contain that unique element. Readers of this book who have little or nothing in the way of scientific/technical qualifications may be encouraged to hear that they are in the company of quite a few successful, established sf writers.

Recognising science fiction's unique element

What is this mysterious ingredient which plays such an important role in deciding what constitutes sf and what doesn't?

Basically, it is *otherness*. I will refine this definition later, but for the moment it is enough to say that otherness is achieved when the author speculates about realities which are in some significant way different from the one we inhabit. The speculation should be done in such a manner that the reader is willing to be carried along with it. *Something odd is going on here*, he should think when being lured into the universe of the story, *and I want to know what it is*.

So important is the element of speculation that some serious workers in the sf field have made attempts to do away with the term 'science fiction' and replace it with 'speculative fiction'. The latter is more appropriate, but the former has been around since the 1920s and we seem to be stuck with it.

Ideally, after a good sf story has ended, the reader will continue thinking about it and will perhaps be encouraged to try taking a mental step further. Most sf devotees are first drawn to the genre in adolescence, and what grips them is that exquisite pleasure which comes when one's mind is being *stretched*.

The author does not necessarily have to be better educated or cleverer than the reader. What he must do, however, is to use all the powers of his creative imagination to force a new trail through the surrounding jungle of possibility. It's hard work, but it can lay claim to being the most exhilarating kind of work there is.

Science fiction versus skiffy

You may be starting to feel that the above is a little abstract and that what's needed is some practical advice with concrete examples. Very well, but having come this far it is worth taking just a little more time to look at another aspect of sf theory. It deals with the difference between science fiction and skiffy – and a good understanding of that difference is of vital importance to the new writer.

The word 'skiffy' was coined only a few years ago and it has an interesting history. As already mentioned, the term 'science fiction' is not particularly popular within the field. It was handed down from the pulp magazines of the inter-war period and has doggedly survived quite a few attempts to replace it. (One contender for a while was 'scientifiction', but that is even worse and can hardly be said to trip off the tongue.)

Unsatisfactory though 'science fiction' may be among the cognoscenti, it is vastly preferred to the interloper 'sci-fi'. This word is loved by newspaper reporters and the media in general – especially by people who cheerfully set themselves up as experts on sf without qualification for doing so, usually in the patronising belief that the field contains very little to be expert about. So much sheer annoyance was caused by the innocuous-seeming little word that, in retaliation, the sf community chose to absorb 'sci-fi' into its own vocabulary. With the pronunciation and spelling modified to 'skiffy', it has come to mean the type of inferior science fiction produced by those who have no insight or empathy with science fiction, and no real grasp of what it is all about.

The reader knows best

I have spent some time on this point because it has a bearing on the new writer's chances of selling his work. Science fiction spent decades in the pulp-magazine ghetto, and even today – no doubt hindered by the recent spate of space pantomimes on the screen – it has not gained a full measure of respect from the literary establishment. It might be too much to say that its dedicated readers are touchy on this point, but they react most unfavourably when served up with a helping of skiffy.

Consider the following plot. A small spaceship, out of fuel, crash-lands near a dome-shaped space colony on an airless planet. Two men in spacesuits get out. One is a member of the Cosmos Police, the other is his prisoner. They have been travelling a long time and are near the limits of their endurance. On reaching the dome they discover it has been struck by a meteorite and all its life-support facilities have been destroyed. A recorded message tells them that replacement equipment will arrive in about twenty days. The men are aware their ship's depleted reserves are down to about thirty man days – which means that only one of them can survive until the rescuers arrive. The policeman proposes a desperate scheme of rationing and complete physical inactivity to eke out the oxygen. The prisoner pretends to go along with the plan, but soon he manages to snatch a weapon and turn it on his captor. In the ensuing duel the prisoner gets shot and killed, and the policeman – although quite seriously wounded – settles down to await the arrival of the supply ship . . .

Question: Is the above an adequate science-fiction plot?

Answer: No. What we have here is a fairly typical example of skiffy.

The main reason it fails as sf is that it is a non-sf story dressed up with the trappings of future space technology. It is what is known in the trade as 'space opera', because the basic plot is equally at home in other genres. The core idea could have been just as easily – and as *completely* – expressed in the form of a Western. The two men could have been a marshal and a bank robber; the dome could have been a remote staging post destroyed by nasty Indians; the oxygen could have been water.

Alternatively, it could have been set in the Sahara desert

and presented as a French Foreign Legion story; or in the South Pacific as a sea adventure; or in the Hindu Kush as a mountain survival yarn.

In all of those cases the essence of the story would have remained the same – the decent, dedicated lawman overcomes adversity to bring in his prisoner. Going back to the given plot example, no amount of scientific jargon, details of advanced weaponry or descriptions of the astronomical environment could change the basic nature of the story. They could disguise it to some extent. Blended in with assiduous skill they might even disguise it enough to fool an inexperienced editor – but the cool, unwavering eye of the perennial sf fan, the paying customer, will not be deceived.

This brings us to the promised refinement of our earlier definition of sf. The vital ingredient of good science fiction is otherness – but it has to be *specific otherness*. A true science-fiction story has as its keystone an imaginative element which cannot be properly expounded in any other literary form.

The fake's progress

It is hard to overemphasise the importance of this point, so I'm going to take a little more space to relate a shameful episode in my own sf writing career.

When you can't win fairly the obvious expedient is to cheat. That's what I often do. Cheating is very popular because it usually brings results, and properly done it is almost an art form in its own right. This book contains many valuable tips on literary cheating, but the following passage is something of a cautionary tale, perhaps even a Dire Warning, about the need for honesty when devising a science-fiction story.

Most writers have had the experience of encountering a published story, the idea of which is so neat, so well formed, so intimately appealing that – after an initial pang of envy – they simply cannot get it out of their minds. That happened to me with an old B-movie in which Robert Ryan plays an ageing boxer. He is overdue for retirement, but keeps on taking the inevitable beatings because he and his wife need the money. Unknown to him, his manager has just received a sizeable bribe from some mobsters who are investing money in promoting a highly unpleasant Golden Boy. It is so long since the hero has won a fight that his manager, being a practical sort, decides there is no point in telling him he is being paid to take a dive, or in sharing the bribe. In the event, the Golden Boy proves so objectionable that the old boxer is inspired to call upon his reserves and give him a good thrashing. The manager, seeing how things are going, disappears with the takings. The mobsters wait outside the arena for the hero, drag him into an alley and smash his hands with bricks, thus putting an end to his boxing career. The ending is actually a happy one because his wife has been on the point of leaving, but now the marriage can be rebuilt.

The story seethed in my brain for years until the ferment became so great that I just had to steal it and pass it off as science fiction. Doing my best to disguise its origins, I moved the setting forward in time to soon after World War III. Atomic radiation had caused mutants to be born, people who had an extra piece of brain tissue on the outside of the skull, on the spot where the fontanelle is on a baby. This lump gave a mutant the power to make anything he imagined visible to others. Mutants were despised, but they could earn a living as entertainers, by projecting vast images of monsters or warriors which did battle with other mutants' creations.

I then wrote my story along the lines of the original plot, with a stark climax in which the mobsters drag the hero into an alley and use a garden spade to shear off his extra brain. Well satisfied with the masterly job of camouflage, I sent the story out under the title of 'Dream Fighter'. It was accepted at once by a leading American sf magazine, and I began congratulating myself on having fooled the sf community. However, my smug pleasure was short-lived.

The first review I saw was in a fan magazine, and it led off with the words: 'This is the oldest boxing story in the world . . .'

New ideas for old

Much of what has been said so far has been somewhat negative in tone, emphasising what science fiction is *not* and advising the new writer of things he should avoid doing. It is a characteristic of writers that when they develop a fondness for one of their story ideas they are loathe to throw it on the scrap heap. So let's take a second look at the plot about the lawman and his prisoner on the airless planet.

The story is as basic as possible for the purpose of illustrating a point, and it has already been rejected as being skiffy – not likely to bring in much in the way of kudos or cash. It has the quality of otherness, but no more than if it had been set in medieval China – in other words, it lacks the specific otherness of true science fiction.

The question now is – can the quality of specific otherness be injected into the story at this late stage? Yes, it can, although this is not the best way to go about such things. As soon as you have had enough practice at evaluating story ideas, you will find yourself instinctively avoiding becoming involved with the ones which fail to measure up to your informed standards. But suppose our little plot has wormed its way into your heart (stranger things happen in the writing business) and you want to build up its strength and send it out to seek its fortune.

The shoot-out at the end offers one possibility. In the first draft you may have equipped the two men with futuristic rayguns, though I hope of a more effective variety than the types used in *Star Wars*, which can only disable bit players and extras. Radiation weapons are popular in sf, but in reality conventional firearms are likely to remain pre-eminent for some time because they are cheap, easy to store and maintain, and are fairly efficient.

Let's go along with that idea and postulate that the lawman has only two weapons – a pistol and a rifle – and that the prisoner manages to grab the latter. Most people know that a rifle can shoot much farther than a pistol, therefore the prisoner is at a great advantage. But wait! The rules about the relative performance of long-barrelled and short-barrelled guns apply on Earth, where there is strong gravity to drag bullets down. In an environment where there was very weak gravity the range of a pistol would be greatly increased.

That simple fact of physics makes possible a twist at the end of the story: the bad guy, believing himself to be well beyond the reach of pistol fire, is careless about taking cover and forfeits his life as a result. As I said earlier, this story is about as basic as it is possible to get – nobody is going to win any awards with it – but in its new version it can at least claim to be science fiction, and not skiffy. The plot ingredient dealing with the effect of low gravity on firearms could not have been used in any other genre. It is specific otherness – the essential element of science fiction.

In the given example the quality of specific otherness

was achieved by challenging one of the reader's most basic assumptions. This is a favourite and well-tried weapon in the sf writer's armoury. There is much more to be said on the subject, but now we are straying into the realm of plotting, which is dealt with in Chapter 3, and it is more important at this stage to continue examining the new writer's approach to his chosen profession.

The importance of market research

'I've written a science-fiction story – can you tell me where I could sell it?'

In all my experience of teaching creative writing and heading writers' workshops, that has probably been the most common question I've been asked.

I get it thrown at me, regularly, and every time I hear it my heart sinks.

There can't be many apprentice writers who haven't been informed of the value of market research, but it seems that many of them fail to assimilate one vital point. *The time to investigate the market is BEFORE you write a story, and not afterwards.*

In most other fields of endeavour that statement would be a platitude, something hardly worth putting into words. It would be a foolhardy individual who decided to pour his time and money into the manufacture of luminous toilet rolls without first checking up on whether there was any public demand for such luxury items. Strangely, though, in the writing field lots of people do the exact equivalent. They place themselves in the position of a tailor who produces a suit and then goes out looking for somebody it will fit.

I have already touched on this matter, but I make no apology for coming back to it. If you want to write for your private satisfaction, like a diarist, that's fine – you don't need to bother with market research; but if you want your work to be published it is only commonsense to take heed of what editors are buying.

The term 'market research' sounds quite daunting, but don't be put off by it. Luckily for us it doesn't involve flooding the streets with clip-boarded interrogators and hiring statisticians to analyse the results. All it means is reading a lot of science fiction. The reading should be done in a fairly systematic way, with an appraising, calculating and self-interested eye – but with no loss of pleasure. (I find it hard to imagine anybody making a success of sf writing without becoming emotionally involved and deriving a lot of sheer enjoyment from the experience.)

Market research – and how to go about it – is so important that it takes up a considerable part of the following chapter. By deciding to read this book you have already shown a canny and commendable interest in the subject. And what about your prospects of eventually getting into print?

Excellent chances of success

The science-fiction field is one in which the market for short stories – both for magazines and anthologies – has remained viable and strong. The demand for novels is also high – sf accounts for about ten per cent of all fiction published today in Great Britain and the USA. And that's before one has even begun to think about radio, television and the cinema. Furthermore, sf editors tend to be more enterprising, more approachable and more sympathetic to new writers than their counterparts in other genres.

I would say that the beginning writer who has taken the trouble to prepare the ground has a far better chance of success in science fiction than in any other branch of literature.

2

A LITERATURE OF IDEAS

Science fiction is often described as a literature of ideas. That definition may be quite comforting to people who have high-powered imaginations, but an unsettling thought may occur even to them. Some ideas can be expounded in as little as three pages, and therefore within the last hundred years or so a staggering amount of them must have been presented to the public gaze by an industrious army of writers. That being the case, is it possible to think up any *new* sf ideas?

The answer generally agreed upon by practitioners in the field is that, although it is theoretically possible, it is most unlikely that anyone, anywhere will come up with a totally new science-fiction idea ever again!

Shock, horror, etc.! Yes, the above statement may seem so outlandish as to be almost a piece of science fiction in itself, but it is a piece of hard information which the beginning writer must assimilate. Doing so will spare him much futile effort and frustration. The view expressed is not defeatist – it is simply a realistic determination of the situation, arrived at after millions of man hours of collective mental effort.

It doesn't mean that a story can no longer have any freshness or novelty value; it is a recognition of the fact that H. G. Wells and a few others who, irritatingly, possessed both a towering imagination and a range of literary skills – arrived on the scene before you did. Subsequent generations of sf writers climbed on their shoulders, ever searching for new ideas or modifying and refining existing ones, and the process continued until we reached today's level of reader sophistication.

The earliest stories by the earliest writers had what we could call primary newness. There was a first time for all the traditional ideas of science fiction. When Wells published his *The War of the Worlds* in 1898 that was *it* as far as the invaders-from-Mars idea was concerned. There was nothing to stop a jealous rival rushing into print with a story about invaders from Venus – but it wouldn't have had the same cachet, would it? The bloom was already off the grape.

The beginning sf writer should not be discouraged by the situation, however. Even though secondary newness is all he can reasonably hope to achieve, it can be very striking and intellectually gratifying. It is a commodity which is in endless supply, gives great scope for ingenuity and subtlety, and which is the stock in trade of every modern sf writer, even the most famous and successful.

One very effective method of achieving secondary newness (I'll simply call it newness from here on) is to take an older idea and stand it on its head. In *The War of the Worlds*, in addition to astounding his readers with the main theme, Wells introduced another idea, one which in my opinion was far more imaginative than interplanetary invaders, and a memorial to his unique genius.

At the end of the book the Martians, having effortlessly defeated the military might of humanity, are laid low by 'humble microbes', carriers of Earthly diseases against which aliens have no immunity.

Now let us jump forward from 1898 to 1961, the year in which Arthur C. Clarke published one of his most effective short stories, 'Before Eden'. The story concerns an explora-

25

tory spaceship from Earth which lands on a comparatively temperate and hospitable Venus. (It was written before NASA space probes really got into their act.) The explorers briefly encounter a beautiful, mosslike primitive life form, then depart for Earth, unaware that they have contaminated Venus's environment with deadly bacteria and viruses. The story concludes with a Biblically poetic sentence: 'Beneath the clouds of Venus, the story of Creation was ended.'

Now, hands up any sf student who has noticed something! Yes, Clarke took the Wells idea and stood it on its head. In the first story, the invaders were wiped out by the germs of another planet; in the second, the germs carried by invaders won the day and wiped out the indigenous life form.

Did Clarke use the inversion technique consciously or unconsciously? I contacted him at his home in Sri Lanka on this point and he said: 'I don't think I was consciously influenced by Wells – but more likely by the talk about contamination, in both directions, that was then worrying NASA – though *The War of the Worlds* may well have been a subconscious influence.'

Whatever way it came about, the point is that Clarke was able to create a successful and memorable story. Once you start that kind of idea-twisting you quickly become adept at it, and it is surprising how far you can go. Sticking with the Wells-Clarke idea, for example, you might decide that the germs carried by the invaders attacked nothing but the *germs* of the other planet, like a cosmic antibiotic, rendering it free of disease.

Where man has gone before

A danger facing the new writer is that his eagerness to plunge into the job may distract him from thinking about the labours of his numerous predecessors. That is why editors continue to receive a high proportion of first-time stories in which a man and a woman go through all kinds of dangers in a spaceship, eventually crash-land on a verdant but uninhabited world, and climb out of the wreckage uttering optimistic dialogue about founding a new race – an exchange which imparts to the reader the 'surprising' news that their names are Adam and Eve. Changing the names to something like Ai'dham and Eeph won't resuscitate that one.

The latest rival to the Adam-and-Eve story features a vast and ferocious space battle which, just when the hero is about to be annihilated, turns out to have been a video game. Older clichés abound in science fiction. The mad scientist (often the sire of a pretty daughter) who wants to destroy the world; the man who goes back in time to ascertain the cause of the Great Fire of London and fails to notice when he drops a lit cigarette end; the nasty invaders of Earth who turn out to be benefactors; the charming visitors from outer space who turn out to be nasty invaders; cute and lovable robots; computers which develop godly powers; evil stellar empires which bear a suspicious resemblance to that of Ancient Rome and whose decline and fall are brought about by tiny groups of freedom fighters; shape-changing aliens of the bodysnatcher variety; flying saucers which can't select better landing places than lonely country roads . . .

The list of clichés is almost endless, and so many of them still make regular appearances – especially in the cinema – that the general public can easily get the impression that there is nothing else to science fiction. This is unfortunate – I think any branch of literature deserves to be judged by its best examples – but to some extent it is something which science-fiction writers have brought on themselves.

British sf writer Christopher Evans has said on the subject of such clichés: 'They represent a fundamental failure of the imagination because the writer has gone for the easy option. The best writers can, of course, breathe fresh life into a hackneyed situation by thinking up new ways to subvert the reader's expectations; but it is a dangerous game for the new writer to play.'

All right, at this stage you are justified in saying: how *do* I get fresh ideas?

Priming the subconscious mind

The first thing is to adopt a positive approach.

It's no good saying to yourself, 'I'm a writer now, and it would be jolly nice if some inspiration were to come along someday.'

You have to play an active, even aggressive, part in the creative process. There is no point in being half-hearted here. You have to make the fact that you are hungry for ideas a part of your mental make-up. If necessary, get the message through to your subconscious by repeating it over and over like a child learning tables. Imagine that you have got your subconscious by the throat, tighten your grip and snarl, 'This is no joke. This is deadly *serious*! I *need* ideas – and you, my friend, are going to supply them.'

Keep telling yourself that you're not a hobbyist, a dabbler, a *flaneur* – you are a writer determined to achieve success, and that your raw material is ideas. When you're in the bath or the dentist's waiting room, or on a boring journey, don't waste time in idle speculation. Remind yourself that you must have ideas; try to think up a new story there and then. I may seem to be laying a huge amount of stress on this point – but that's because it is vital. If you don't get your subconscious properly primed and fully aware of what is expected of it, nothing much will happen.

Happily, it isn't necessary to keep the indoctrination at such an intense pitch for very long. Within a few days or a week your commands should have percolated down into the lower levels of your mind, and from then on only an occasional reinforcement will be required to keep the creative machinery running. You won't feel much different in everyday life, but ideas will begin to pop into the forefront of your mind, regularly and dependably.

I'm aware that I talking about the subconscious as though it were a physical organ, something we know all about and can tinker with like a carburettor. In fact, if such a Freudian entity exists at all, the subconscious mind is an abstract object of impenetrable mystery. I don't know what goes on down there – neither does anybody else – but I do know that the discipline described above actually achieves results.

Brownies in action

Recently I was chatting with a friend who had just been through an unpleasant experience – a hotel lift she was in had dropped a couple of floors before the emergency brake gripped. While describing the incident she said, 'My whole life flashed before my eyes.'

Now, I don't know how many times I've heard those words over the years, but on that particular occasion something went *ping*! in a basement of my mind. *What if people's lives really do flash before their eyes in the few seconds before sudden death?* I wondered. *Suppose that it isn't just in the form of some blurred images. Imagine it is a crystal-clear*

29

review of key scenes from life, seen with absolute detail and clarity. Furthermore, imagine that a man is committing suicide by jumping off a tall building because a friend has betrayed him. How would he feel if – just before he hit the ground – one of those diamond-sharp images revealed that he had made a mistake, that his friend had been faithful to him all along, and that he had thrown his life away for nothing?

The idea was fairly lightweight – not worth more than a few thousand words – but it had a neatness to it which appealed to me. I put it in the notebook, went home and began writing the story almost immediately. It took about two days. On its first outing it sold to a major anthology for a decent fee, and soon afterwards was also taken by a television film company. My subconscious had obeyed my standing order, you see. It had performed its appointed task, and as a result my income for two days' work went well into four figures – and all because a friend had uttered a commonplace remark!

I find the process of inspiration quite astonishing. Especially when a complete story idea springs into the mind there is an eerie feeling of having received a gift from elsewhere. Many authors of prose and poetry have commented on the same phenomenon.

Robert Louis Stevenson said that most of the ideas which came to him were the work of his Brownies – little folk who worked in the depths of his mind. When going to bed at night he 'no longer sought amusement but printable and profitable tales' and when he had dozed off, his 'Little People contrived their evolutions with the same mercantile design.'

Writing is a lonely profession, so it's nice to be able to play with the notion that you have a little band of eager helpers who will beaver away on your behalf even when you're asleep.

Reading sf for fun and profit

It is unlikely, however, that Stevenson would have come up with the idea of his Jekyll and Hyde classic had he not been doing some conscious thinking about the duality of human nature. For similar reasons, it is advisable for the beginning sf writer to do as much reading in the field as he can. The subconscious has to work on what the conscious hands down to it. That's why a good engineer will dream up a way of improving gearboxes and not a new design for curtain material.

Diligent reading of science fiction has a number of beneficial effects. The ideas you encounter will help spark off ideas of your own, and it will also help you to avoid expending time and effort on ideas which may seem excitingly new to you, but which have already been done to death.

Obviously there is a problem with the fact that so many ideas and variants and sub-variants have already been worked over. Until around 1950 it was possible for the real devotee to have read all the science fiction that had ever been published, and to keep up with all that was then being published. Those days are over, but the situation is far from hopeless, because extensive reading not only exposes you to ideas – it makes you familiar with *classes of ideas*.

After a while, when you have got the general feel of things, you will be able to make an objective assessment of your own ideas as they appear. 'No,' you may say, 'this one is *bound* to have been done before.' Or, 'This one *might* have been done before, but not very often, and if I add some judicious modifications . . .' Or, on a good day, 'This is *it*! I've struck pay dirt!'

Are you sitting comfortably?

Clearly, the sort of research I'm talking about will require some effort, but the apprentice science-fiction writer is singularly lucky in the amount of organised material which is conveniently available. I hate to think of the sheer quantity of auxiliary work which would have to be done if one wanted to bone up to a respectable and useful level on, say, the detective story or the Western.

In science fiction, however, most of the time-consuming work has already been done for you. The field abounds in comprehensive anthologies which almost seem to have been compiled solely for the benefit of new writers. The earliest was *Popular Romances*, edited by Henry Weber in 1812, but that is of more value to literary historians than writers. For our purposes, the most important of the front-runners was *Adventures in Time and Space*, edited by Raymond J. Healy and J. Francis McComas in 1946, and containing 35 stories in 997 pages. Anybody who reads it cannot help but gain a broad understanding of much that is going on in modern science fiction. Some of the best anthologies of the last five decades are mentioned in the appendix.[1]

In addition, some major sf publishers conscientiously maintain retrospective lists which keep the field's most classic and seminal novels readily available. Another bonus for the new writer is the existence of comprehensive reference works, lovingly and expertly written, which provide almost as much in the way of sheer entertainment as they do in relevant education.[2]

Finally in this section – and I can't imagine a similar facility in any other genre – there are specialist mail-order firms run by genuine, old-fashioned, dyed-in-the-wool book-lovers, whose knowledge is encyclopaedic and enthusiasm boundless.[3] They send their customers regular lists of new and second-hand publications, and take a justifiable pride in their ability to find rare or obscure works.

Thanks to them, it doesn't matter if you live in the Shetlands or the Falklands or the wilds of deepest Buckinghamshire – you can get hold of what you need.

You don't have to be a hermit

Writing, as writers keep saying, is a lonely occupation – but it isn't necessary to eschew company during the initial creative process. It can be very useful to sit down with carefully chosen friends and – as it is referred to in the trade – 'bounce ideas around.' Major British sf writer James White and I used to work in the same firm, and one of the things we most enjoyed was our lunchtime ideas session.

One of us would float an embryo new idea, or outline a problem which had brought progress in a current story to a grinding halt, and then we would set to. These meetings were highly productive, but the strange thing we discovered was that neither of us received from the other any kind of suggestion that was directly useful. What did happen, though, was that hearing fresh notions from an outsider's viewpoint stimulated our own creative centres. New ideas were developed, problems were solved, and James and I believe those sessions were important in our early careers.

A word of warning here! You don't have to be a hermit while preparing for a story, but it is important not to be a blabbermouth either. Let's say you have found a decent idea and have built up a good plot from it – do not make the mistake of relating the whole thing to your family or friends, or even an acquaintance in the pub. Pleasant though such oratory may be, it is dangerous in that you perform the storyteller's act and receive your audience reaction, and something inside you is satisfied. The literary mainspring inside you unwinds slightly each time the story is expounded, and if you keep doing it there is a good chance that the story will never reach the manuscript stage.

Even if you do finally write it, your attack will be blunted; something ineffable but important will be missing. I could always tell when James White made a creative breakthrough during one of our talk sessions – he immediately clammed up and refused to discuss the idea any further. And he always picked up the same signal from me.

It is vital that you hold something back, something that you particularly cherish, nourishing yourself on visions of all the excitement there will be when it is finally unleashed *in print* on an astonished world. Yes, be a secret megalomaniac about it. All writers are egotists to some degree, whether they admit it or not, and it is this gleeful anticipation of future triumphs which keeps them going when the silent hours are long and lonely, the fingers are hesitant on the keyboard, and the vista of back-garden clothes lines seems more than usually uninspiring.

Here's a personal illustration of the importance I attach to this matter. Like most full-time sf writers, I sell a novel in advance of writing it, on the basis of a detailed synopsis. Obviously, it's very much in my interests for the synopsis to be as persuasive as possible so that I will win a contract and go on having a roof over my head. But, even in those circumstances, *I invariably hold something back!*

There has to be some artistic element, some ingenious aspect, some ultimate flourish, the knowledge of which will remain mine and mine alone until that day when the first reader opens the first copy. Admittedly, the reader does not always recognise or appreciate this literary treat when he finally gets to sample it, but the main thing is that it has done its work on my behalf.

How 'heavy' is an idea?

As soon as you've got a good idea and have satisfied yourself that you want to turn it into a finished story, it is worth making a rough estimate of how long the story will be. This should be done at an early stage because it has a bearing on how you go about plotting the yarn. It is a waste of time to devise nests of sub-plots for a piece which is going to make six pages; on the other hand, a long work is going to seem a bit sparse and spindly without some layers of plot complexity.

After a bit of practice you will soon acquire the art of weighing up an idea and pacing yourself as you write it, especially if you are doing your required reading and seeing what others have done in this respect. A common mistake among beginners – anxious to succeed by giving value for money – is to cram too much into a given space. (Regrettably, almost as common is the tendency for old hands at the game to do the opposite.)

If, as a new writer, you feel impelled to keep packing more and more goodies into the literary picnic hamper, remember that the reader feels disappointed when his pleasure is brought to a premature end. If a story is overlong it is always possible to do some judicious skimming, but if it is too short there is nothing that can be done and the paying customer will have a feeling of being let down or stranded.

Those damned readers! They frequently masquerade as ordinary Joes, plain punters, Mr Man-In-The-Street – then they confound us by coming up with sophisticated value judgements about things like pacing, technicalities which we as wordsmiths know to be our private domain. I was an avid reader as a child, and can remember – even then – being totally engrossed in a story when, out of the blue, would come a sudden anxiety, a disturbing and illusion-shattering thought. *Is there enough left*? I would leaf through to the end of the story, being careful not to read the last few lines, and only when reassured that there was indeed enough space for a satisfactory conclusion would I relax again. It just goes to show – you have to respect the reader and never, even when trying to be generous with ideas, short-change him in this matter of word length.

Stories are categorised according to length. It is only to be expected that in the literary world at large there will be some vagueness of boundary and definition, but in science fiction – perhaps because of a fondness for rationality – things tend to be more organised.

Of the many sf awards presented each year the most prestigious are the Nebula and the Hugo, and for their judging panels there is no discretion at all as regards category and length.

A short story is not more than 7,500 words long; a novelette runs between 7,500 and 17,500; a novella between 17,500 and 40,000; and anything over 40,000 constitutes a novel.

The short story is often the most attractive form for the new sf writer, for obvious reasons, and was the means of entry into the profession for most of today's top authors. As we have established, a story should always be written to its natural length, but it is useful to know how the different fiction categories are decided. If you have the ambition to collect a big award with one of your early efforts – and why not? – it is worth noting that a story of, say, 7,700 words, which you regard as a short, would be going into the arena against more muscular opponents with a top weight of up to 17,500 words. As in boxing, where the contestant who is closest to the maximum weight allowed in his class is usually the more likely to win, a short story of 7,400 words has a better chance than one of 800, all other things being equal.

There is also the question of awkward lengths. A story

of 38,000 words would not quite qualify as a novel, and also could be difficult for the new writer to sell to a magazine. The editor might feel it was a tricky decision, allocating such a large proportion of his space to an untried author.

From idea to plot

I'm not proposing that you should think in numerical detail about story lengths at this stage – it is enough to have a general awareness that the categories exist and can impinge on your work. Having got hold of a promising idea – one that *feels* good to you – the next step is to build a plot which does your idea justice.

3

PLOTTING

One of the most basic mistakes the new sf writer can make is to confuse the *idea* for a story with the *plot* for the same story.

It is quite natural and understandable that in the heat of inspiration the tyro, eager to launch into his career, will rush to the desk and begin writing. But, without his having done the necessary preliminary work, the result is very often unsatisfactory. What tends to come out is a small handful of scrappy scenes hinged around the central idea. They can be well handled in themselves, but the whole assemblage is shaky, too short, not capable of going anywhere. Even the author, doting parent though he is, usually can't help but feel that his brainchild has failed to live up to expectations, although he may not be able to diagnose the trouble.

An idea can be compared to a precious stone in that it has various attractive qualities which must be seen from different angles. A plot is then a machine, like something in a jeweller's window, which holds the diamond up to the light and turns it this way and that, sparking fire off every facet, ensuring that all of its best features are well displayed.

I'm sorry if the above metaphor has become elaborate, but it is such a good and accurate analogy that it deserves a short paragraph to itself. Your ideas *are* precious; they have more than one valuable attribute, and it is damned well up to you to make sure that each and every one of them is brought to the reader's attention. Nobody else is going to do it for you, and it isn't going to happen by accident.

I can become quite heated on this subject because a lack of plotting know-how is a major cause of literary disappointment. Not only does the aspiring writer have his hopes dashed – the rest of us are deprived of the pleasure we could have had from seeing his stories in print.

Inspiration and perspiration

At the beginning of this chapter I used the phrase 'necessary preliminary work'. The work referred to really *is* work, even though it can be more enjoyable than any sport, and there is no way of telling in advance just how much will be required to shape a finished, commercially viable plot. It could be as little as ten minutes' worth, especially for a skilled practitioner, or it could add up to many hours.

The principal unknown factor is in the nature of the idea itself. Some ideas are essentially lightweight, and the educated instinct will quickly provide strong indications of what is possible. Other ideas, however, have a thrilling sense of depth and near-endless potential. Some will yield plot after useful plot, and – even after the author has selected and sold the one he judges the best – he may be left with a nagging suspicion that he could have done better with some extra effort, that a major award or a movie contract may have gone begging.

At the centre of this chapter is a reprint of my most successful short story, 'Light Of Other Days'. It has been anthologised about *forty* times, and – although only 3,000 words long – has earned more money than one could reasonably expect from a novel. Naturally, I'm quite tickled with that achievement, but the rewards didn't simply drop into my lap.

After getting the initial idea I spent *two years* turning it around in my mind before sitting down to write. It wasn't two years of full-time pondering and brain-racking, of course, but I put in many hours in train stations and the like, thinking up and rejecting plot after plot, striving for *the* plot – the one which would do full justice to my cherished idea.

I will analyse 'Light of Other Days' and its genesis in full, but before that there is more to be said about basic plotting in science fiction and how to go about it.

I want to tell you a story

It has already been said that in a science-fiction story the central idea is very important, so much so that it has to be accorded the status of a major character. It follows, therefore, that the plot structure – the development of the idea – will be of equal consequence.

In the mainstream literary establishment it is customary to look down one's nose at strong plotting. The idea seems to be that a 'proper' piece of writing has so many fine qualities – style, erudition, insight into the human condition, etc. – that a compelling story line is superfluous, flashy, not quite the done thing. This feeling is so strong that in some cases the serious writer, fearful that some element of suspense might creep into his narrative, takes the precaution of putting the end of his story at the beginning.

Yet, in spite of all that has been said against it, the strongly plotted story – the type that stimulates interest and a desire to find out what happens next – continues to be highly popular with the general reading public. When the average reader is asked to say why he has a fondness for a particular story he will usually begin by relating the plot and saying how intrigued he was by it. Often he will not even bother to mention other attributes such as prose style or depth of characterisation. That doesn't mean those qualities made no contribution to his enjoyment of the story. They may have played a much greater part than he consciously realises, but in his mind the plot *is* the story.

Well-plotted stories also remain popular with editors, because they know what is in demand from their readers; but more important to us at the moment are the benefits a strong, tightly constructed plot confers upon the writer.

When I began writing short stories I found the plotting extremely difficult, and sometimes – in my eagerness to get going – would settle for a plot which I knew to be a bit weak, to sag a little in the middle. 'That's all right,' I would say. 'When I come to that bit I'll gloss over it by doing a bit of extra-special writing – dazzle the reader with stylistic fireworks, throw in a touch of the old deathless prose.'

That was self-deception of the worst kind, even had I had enough literary skill to pull off the trick. Firstly, because a writer should *always* be doing his best – otherwise he is wasting his time and talent; secondly, the reader is not so easily fooled. On the other hand, when you sit down to write a story and you *know* that it has a neat, solid, water-tight plot, your confidence is boosted. You feel that you are on a winner right from the start, and the accompanying elation sustains you during the most difficult patches.

There was an Englishman, an Irishman and a Martian . . .

For the mainstream writer the classic approach to creating a story is to bring a handful of characters together, let them interact, and then describe what happens. This method isn't much use to the science-fiction writer. If he tries it nothing much will happen – that is to say, nothing much of interest to the science-fiction reader.

It is much more effective for the sf writer to invert the traditional method, to start off with an idea and invent a set of characters which will enable him to exploit it to the full. In science fiction the range of possibilities in any given situation is much greater than in ordinary fiction, so this method can be very fruitful.

Remember our two characters – the lawman and his prisoner – whom we left stranded on that airless asteroid back in Chapter 1? Those poor souls have been stuck there so long that I have begun to feel slightly guilty about the whole thing. In fact, I've begun to develop a sneaking affection for them. Whimsical though that may sound, it is a fairly common phenomenon with authors and, within reasonable limits, is something to be encouraged. Your characters, even the lowliest spear-carriers, *should* take on a life of their own in your mind. This helps with characterisation, but it also has a bearing on plotting because sometimes you will find it difficult to make even a minor figure do what you want him to do. It is a sign that your trusty servant, the subconscious, is becoming involved, and that you really are doing your job as a creative writer.

On this subject, top British sf writer John Brunner says: 'You should be guided by your characters. After all, you're an outsider in their universe – they actually *live* in it.'

All right – as an exercise in basic plotting we are going to return to the asteroid. It will help us to think of the two characters as rounded human beings if they have names, so let's dub them Benny (benefactor) and Mal (malefactor).

Playing by the rules

The last time we saw them, Benny had just overcome Mal because in an environment with very little gravity a pistol will shoot much farther than on Earth. That's fine, but in good sf – just as in a good mystery – there are certain ground rules which must be observed. If Agatha P. D. Rendell had written a story whose denouement revolved around poison being secreted in the sac of a fountain pen, she would have been obliged in the course of the narrative to make prominent mention of the pen and its availability at the scene of the crime. Her readers would have risen in rebellion if the pen had suddenly popped up in the last couple of pages. Going further, if Agatha had been in the mood for demonstrating her mastery of her trade – i.e. showing off – she might have slipped in an early scene in which somebody tried to write with the pen and was annoyed by the wateriness of the ink.

The same kind of rules apply in science fiction. In the case of Benny and Mal, the reader would be justifiably irritated if it were only in the final paragraph or so that he learned about the lack of gravity. In this type of story, the more radical your contradiction of the reader's presuppositions, the more scrupulous you have to be about preparing the ground. You are required to play fair, to supply a decent amount of legitimate hints. If you don't, the reader who has been deceived will cry, 'That's a cheat!' If you do play the game, however, the outcome can only be in your favour. Should the reader fail to see what's coming he will be impressed by your ingenuity; and if he does manage to outguess you with some effort he will be pleased by his *own* ingenuity, and, human nature being what it is, will become an even greater admirer of your work.

Going back to Benny and Mal: if you check the initial outline of the plot you will see that it specifies the scene of the action as an 'airless planet'. That was fine for the old skiffy version of the plot, but it will not do for the improved new draft in which minuscule gravity plays a vital part. It is necessary to shift the action to an asteroid. Anybody with even a wisp of astronomy knows that an asteroid is a very small body, and therefore has practically no gravity – so by changing the locale you have kept faith with yourself.

But there's more to it than that!

With any other ending in mind it would be enough to make a casual mention of the fact that the story was set on an asteroid. It and its special physical conditions would not need more than a few lines in the routine description of the story's setting. With the low-gravity ending, however, you are required to seed the narrative with the above-mentioned legitimate hints. These might include references to the difficulty of walking with a dignified gait, the slowness with which something falls to the ground, and so on. The number of hints is up to you. If you concentrate on being really skilful and subtle and devious, you could risk putting in quite a few. In general, the more you get away with the more impressed the reader will be, but you have to weigh up the chances of failure very carefully.

An eagle's eye view

As you have seen, I advocate a cerebral and calculating approach to plotting. Ideally, one would be able to conceive a good plot and thrash out every last detail before writing the first sentence of the MS. But, especially in longer works, that is not always possible. There is a limit to how far you can see ahead – even if you have the mind of a Russian chess champion.

Let's say that, in the case of Benny and Mal, you had already written a draft of the skiffy version before enlightenment came, and now you are going to revise it. Avoid making the revision merely cosmetic. You will need to 'back-plot', i.e. to read the story again with a fierce, unforgiving eye and excise every remnant of the old plot which conflicts with or detracts from the new one. That is easier said than done, because elements of the first version may have wormed their way into your thinking and can be difficult to dislodge.

For example, Benny and Mal were on their way to a space outpost, which would be quite a reasonable thing to find on a full-scale planet. But what is it doing perched on a mere asteroid? The conscientious sf writer will not neglect that question, because it affects the logical underpinning of the story. Even if the reader doesn't consciously raise the objection, it could subliminally mar his suspension of disbelief and leave him with a nagging feeling that something was wrong.

The story we are working upon would hardly sell in the adult market, but it could possibly be bought for juveniles or 'kidults' – and young people can be just as discerning as grown-ups, or even more so.

It would not be necessary – in fact it would be undesirable – to spend a lot of wordage justifying the presence of a habitat on a small asteroid. You could give the asteroid a core of some incredibly precious mineral, in which case the habitat would become a mining station. Perhaps the asteroid is well placed for the study of some astronomical event, in which case it would support an observatory; perhaps it is in a region where radio signals are hampered, in which case it could be a communications relay station.

The trained sf imagination can keep on producing variations like that, and they don't have to be for background use. Suppose we decide that the low-gravity shoot-out plot is a bit too raw and needs to be taken further. This is exactly where science fiction offers its writers creative scope, far more than is available in the mainstream.

Mal's motive for trying to kill Benny is that between them they only have enough oxygen for fifteen days, and it will be twenty days before new supplies arrive. Let's go to work on that lump of raw material with one of our most trusted tools: the technique of undermining the reader's assumptions.

When Mal set out to kill Benny *he* was assuming that Benny depended upon oxygen as much as he did – but what if Benny, completely normal though he appeared, was not an ordinary human being? What if he turned out to be a product of biological engineering, one adapted for space travel, a man who could live on almost no oxygen? Mal, who may not be such a bad guy after all, might find this out after he had succeeded in murdering Benny, and then could be consumed with remorse. He had killed because he thought it was necessary for his own survival – and now, not only does he feel terrible, he has to go up for murder as well as robbery.

Let's keep twisting and inverting. Mal – who is turning out to be quite a nice person – has succeeded only in wounding Benny, but his bullet has punctured Benny's spacesuit and death will quickly follow. Mal, realising he could never take a human life, rushes to repair the suit. Then, in atonement for his evil ways, he disconnects his own oxygen tank and keels over, ready to die. To his surprise, he is resuscitated by Benny, who reveals the true situation to him. Now, not only does Mal feel good, but the robbery charge against him is going to be dropped because of his heroism.

Everything is now sweetness and light. Or is it? What if Benny's engineered biological system does indeed use very little oxygen when it is in good shape, but in the event of being damaged, say by a bullet, starts burning oxygen up much *faster* than an ordinary human being? What if Benny himself has just discovered that alarming fact? Is he a good guy right down to his boots, or will he be tempted to dispose of Mal to preserve his own life?

Is your head starting to spin? I confess that mine is. We started off with a deliberately simple and unsophisticated little yarn, applied some sf plotting techniques in what was meant to be a pure classroom demonstration, and now – all of a sudden – we're dealing with a story which has the potential to sell in almost any market, and which I would quite like to write someday. Unless a reader of this book beats me to it, that is . . .

Plotting in practice

Now I want to introduce you to that short story I mentioned earlier, the one which has been anthologised so many times. In contrast to the saga of Benny and Mal, it is set on Earth only a short distance in the future, and there is no physical action to speak of. The action is in an interplay of emotion and the unveiling of an idea, which meant that the success of the story was even more dependent on very careful, meticulous plotting.

Light of Other Days

Leaving the village behind, we followed the heady
sweeps of the road up into a land of slow glass.

I had never seen one of the farms before and at first
found them slightly eerie – an effect heightened by
imagination and circumstance. The car's turbine was
pulling smoothly and quietly in the damp air so that we
seemed to be carried over the convolutions of the road
in a kind of supernatural silence. On our right the
mountain sifted down into a perfect valley of timeless
pine, and everywhere stood the great frames of slow
glass, drinking light. An occasional flash of afternoon
sunlight on their wind bracing created an illusion of
movement, but in fact the frames were deserted. The
rows of windows had been standing on the hillside for
years, staring into the valley, and men only cleaned
them in the middle of the night when their human
presence would not matter to the thirsty glass.

They were fascinating, but Selina and I didn't mention the windows. I think we hated each other so much
we both were reluctant to sully anything new by draw-
ing it into the nexus of our emotions. The holiday, I
had begun to realize, was a stupid idea in the first place.
I had thought it would cure everything, but, of course,
it didn't stop Selina being pregnant and, worse still,
it didn't even stop her being angry about being pregnant.

Rationalizing our dismay over her condition, we had
circulated the usual statements to the effect that we
would have liked having children – but later on, at the
proper time. Selina's pregnancy had cost us her well-
paid job and with it the new house we had been nego-
tiating and which was far beyond the reach of my
income from poetry. But the real source of our annoy-

ance was that we were face to face with the realization that people who say they want children later always mean they want children never. Our nerves were thrumming with the knowledge that we, who had thought ourselves so unique, had fallen into the same biological trap as every mindless rutting creature which ever existed.

The road took us along the southern slopes of Ben Cruachan until we began to catch glimpses of the grey Atlantic far ahead. I had just cut our speed to absorb the view better when I noticed the sign spiked to a gatepost. It said: 'SLOW GLASS – Quality High, Prices Low – J. R. Hagan.' On an impulse I stopped the car on the verge, wincing slightly as tough grasses whipped noisily at the bodywork.

'Why have we stopped?' Selina's neat, smoke-silver head turned in surprise.

'Look at that sign. Let's go up and see what there is. The stuff might be reasonably priced out here.'

Selina's voice was pitched high with scorn as she refused, but I was too taken with my idea to listen. I had an illogical conviction that doing something extravagant and crazy would set us right again.

'Come on,' I said, 'the exercise might do us some good. We've been driving too long anyway.'

She shrugged in a way that hurt me and got out of the car. We walked up a path made of irregular, packed clay steps nosed with short lengths of sapling. The path curved through trees which clothed the edge of the hill and at its end we found a low farmhouse. Beyond the little stone building tall frames of slow glass gazed out towards the voice-stilling sight of Cruachan's ponderous descent towards the waters of Loch Linnhe. Most of the panes were perfectly transparent but a few were dark, like panels of polished ebony.

As we approached the house through a neat cobbled yard a tall middle-aged man in ash-coloured tweeds rose and waved to us. He had been sitting on a low rubble wall which bounded the yard, smoking a pipe and staring towards the house. At the front window of the cottage a young woman in a tangerine dress stood with a small boy in her arms, but she turned disinterestedly and moved out of sight as we drew near.

'Mr Hagan?' I guessed.

'Correct. Come to see some glass, have you? Well, you've come to the right place.' Hagan spoke crisply, with traces of the pure Highland accent which sounds so much like Irish to the unaccustomed ear. He had one of those calmly dismayed faces one finds on elderly road-menders and philosophers.

'Yes,' I said. 'We're on holiday. We saw your sign.'

Selina, who usually has a natural fluency with strangers, said nothing. She was looking towards the now empty window with what I thought was a slightly puzzled expression.

'Up from London, are you? Well, as I said, you've come to the right place – and at the right time too. My wife and I don't see many people this early in the season.'

I laughed. 'Does that mean we might be able to buy a little glass without mortgaging our home?'

'Look at that now,' Hagan said, smiling helplessly. 'I've thrown away any advantage I might have had in the transaction. Rose, that's my wife, says I never learn. Still, let's sit down and talk it over.' He pointed at the rubble wall then glanced doubtfully at Selina's immaculate blue skirt. 'Wait till I fetch a rug from the house.' Hagan limped quickly into the cottage, closing the door behind him.

'Perhaps it wasn't such a marvellous idea to come up here,' I whispered to Selina, 'but you might at least be pleasant to the man. I think I can smell a bargain.'

'Some hope,' she said with deliberate coarseness. 'Surely even you must have noticed that ancient dress his wife is wearing? He won't give much away to strangers.'

'Was that his wife?'

'Of course that was his wife.'

'Well, well,' I said surprised. 'Anyway, try to be civil with him, I don't want to be embarrassed.'

Selina snorted, but she smiled whitely when Hagan reappeared and I relaxed a little. Strange how a man can love a woman and yet at the same time pray for her to fall under a train.

Hagan spread the tartan blanket on the wall and we sat down, feeling slightly self-conscious at having been translated from our city-oriented lives into a rural tableau. On the distant slate of the Loch, beyond the watchful frames of slow glass, a slow-moving steamer drew a white line towards the south. The boisterous mountain air seemed almost to invade our lungs, giving us more oxygen than we required.

'Some of the glass farmers around here,' Hagan began, 'give strangers, such as yourselves, a sales talk about how beautiful the autumn is in this part of Argyll. Or it might be the spring, or the winter. I don't do that – any fool knows that a place which doesn't look right in summer never looks right. What do you say?'

I nodded compliantly.

'I want you just to take a good look out towards Mull, Mr . . .'

'Garland.'

'. . . Garland. That's what you're buying if you buy my glass, and it never looks better than it does at this minute. The glass is in perfect phase, none of it is less than ten years thick – and a four-foot window will cost you two hundred pounds.'

'*Two hundred*,' Selina said, shocked. 'That's as much as they charge at the Scenedow shop in Bond Street.'

Hagan smiled patiently, then looked closely at me to see if I knew enough about glass to appreciate what he had been saying. His price had been much higher than I had hoped – but *ten years thick!* The cheap glass one found in places like Vistaplex and Pane-o-rama stores usually consisted of a quarter of an inch of ordinary glass faced with a veneer of slow glass perhaps only ten or twelve months thick.

'You don't understand, darling,' I said, already determined to buy. 'This glass will last ten years and it's in phase.'

'Doesn't that only mean it keeps time?'

Hagan smiled at her again, realizing he had no further necessity to bother with me. 'Only, you say! Pardon me, Mrs Garland, but you don't seem to appreciate the miracle, the genuine honest-to-goodness miracle, of engineering precision needed to produce a piece of glass in phase. When I say the glass is ten years thick it means it takes light ten years to pass through it. In effect, each one of those panes is ten light-years thick – more than twice the distance to the nearest star – so a variation in actual thickness of only a millionth of an inch would . . .'

He stopped talking for a moment and sat quietly looking towards the house. I turned my head from the view of the Loch and saw the young woman standing at the window again. Hagan's eyes were filled with a kind of greedy reverence which made me feel uncomfortable and at the same time convinced me Selina had been wrong. In my experience husbands never looked at wives that way, at least, not at their own.

The woman remained in view for a few seconds, dress glowing warmly, then moved back into the room. Suddenly I received a distinct, though inexplicable, impression she was blind. My feeling was that Selina and I were perhaps blundering through an emotional interplay as violent as our own.

'I'm sorry,' Hagan continued, 'I thought Rose was going to call me for something. Now, where was I, Mrs Garland? Ten light-years compressed into a quarter of an inch means . . .'

I ceased to listen, partly because I was already sold, partly because I had heard the story of slow glass many times before and had never yet understood the principles involved. An acquaintance with scientific training had once tried to be helpful by telling me to visualize a pane of slow glass as a hologram which did not need coherent light from a laser for the reconstitution of its visual information, and in which every photon of ordinary light passed through a spiral tunnel coiled outside the radius of capture of each atom in the glass. This gem of, to me, incomprehensibility not only told me nothing, it convinced me once again that a mind as non-technical as mine should concern itself less with causes than effects.

The most important effect, in the eyes of the average individual, was that light took a long time to pass through a sheet of slow glass. A new piece was always jet black because nothing had yet come through, but one could stand the glass beside, say, a woodland lake until the scene emerged, perhaps a year later. If the glass was then removed and installed in a dismal city flat, the flat would – for that year – appear to overlook the woodland lake. During the year it wouldn't be merely a very realistic but still picture – the water would ripple in sunlight, silent animals would come to drink, birds would cross the sky, night would follow day, season would follow season. Until one day, a year later, the beauty held in the subatomic pipelines would be exhausted and the familiar grey cityscape would reappear.

Apart from its stupendous novelty value, the commercial success of slow glass was founded on the fact that having a scenedow was the exact emotional equivalent of owning land. The meanest cave dweller could look out on misty parks – and who was to say they weren't his? A man who really owns tailored gardens and estates doesn't spend his time proving his ownership by crawling on his ground, feeling, smelling, tasting it. All he receives from the land are light patterns, and with scenedows those patterns could be taken into coal mines, submarines, prison cells.

On several occasions I have tried to write short pieces about the enchanted crystal but, to me, the theme is so ineffably poetic as to be, paradoxically, beyond the reach of poetry – mine at any rate. Besides, the best songs and verse had already been written, with prescient inspiration by men who had died long before slow glass was discovered. I had no hope of equalling, for example, Moore with his:

> *Oft in the stilly night,*
> *Ere slumber's chain has bound me,*
> *Fond Memory brings the light,*
> *Of other days around me . . .*

It took only a few years for slow glass to develop from a scientific curiosity to a sizeable industry. And much to the astonishment of us poets – those of us who remain convinced that beauty lives though lilies die – the trappings of that industry were no different from those of any other. There were good scenedows which cost a lot of money, and there were inferior scenedows which cost rather less. The thickness, measured in years, was an important factor in the cost but there was also the question of *actual* thickness, or phase.

Even with the most sophisticated engineering techniques available, thickness control was something of a hit-and-miss affair. A coarse discrepancy could mean that a pane intended to be five years thick might be five and a half, so that light which entered in summer emerged in winter; a fine discrepancy could mean that noon sunshine emerged at midnight. These incompatibilities had their peculiar charm – many night workers, for example, liked having their own private time zones – but, in general, it cost more to buy scenedows which kept closely in step with real time.

Selina still looked unconvinced when Hagan had finished speaking. She shook her head almost imperceptibly and I knew he had been using the wrong approach. Quite suddenly the pewter helmet of her hair was disturbed by a cool gust of wind, and huge clean tumbling drops of rain began to spang round us from an almost cloudless sky.

'I'll give you a cheque now,' I said abruptly, and saw Selina's green eyes triangulate angrily on my face. 'You can arrange delivery?'

'Aye, delivery's no problem,' Hagan said, getting to his feet. 'But wouldn't you rather take the glass with you?'

'Well, yes – if you don't mind.' I was shamed by his readiness to trust my scrip.

'I'll unclip a pane for you. Wait here. It won't take

long to slip it into a carrying frame.' Hagan limped down the slope towards the seriate windows, through some of which the view towards Linnhe was sunny, while others were cloudy and a few pure black.

Selina drew the collar of her blouse close at her throat. 'The least he could have done was invite us inside. There can't be so many fools passing through that he can afford to neglect them.'

I tried to ignore the insult and concentrated on writing the cheque. One of the outsize drops broke across my knuckles, splattering the pink paper.

'All right,' I said, 'let's move in under the eaves till he gets back.' You bitch, I thought, as I felt the whole thing go completely wrong. I just had to be a fool to marry you. A prize fool, a fool's fool – and now that you've trapped part of me inside you I'll never ever, never ever, *never ever* get away.

Feeling my stomach clench itself painfully, I ran behind Selina to the side of the cottage. Beyond the window the neat living room, with its coal fire, was empty but the child's toys were scattered on the floor. Alphabet blocks and a wheelbarrow the exact colour of freshly pared carrots. As I stared in, the boy came running from the other room and began kicking the blocks. He didn't notice me. A few moments later the young woman entered the room and lifted him, laughing easily and whole-heartedly as she swung the boy under her arm. She came to the window as she had done earlier. I smiled self-consciously, but neither she nor the child responded.

My forehead pricked icily. *Could they both be blind?* I sidled away.

Selina gave a little scream and I spun towards her.

'The rug!' she said. 'It's getting soaked.'

She ran across the yard in the rain, snatched the

reddish square from the dappling wall and ran back, towards the cottage door. Something heaved convulsively in my subconscious.

'Selina,' I shouted. 'Don't open it!'

But it was too late. She had pushed open the latched wooden door and was standing, hand over mouth, looking into the cottage. I moved close to her and took the rug from her unresisting fingers.

As I was closing the door I let my eyes traverse the cottage's interior. The neat living room in which I had just seen the woman and child was, in reality, a sickening clutter of shabby furniture, old newspapers, cast-off clothing and smeared dishes. It was damp, stinking and utterly deserted. The only object I recognized from my view through the window was the little wheelbarrow, paintless and broken.

I latched the door firmly and ordered myself to forget what I had seen. Some men who live alone are good housekeepers; others just don't know how.

Selina's face was white. 'I don't understand. I don't understand it.'

'Slow glass works both ways,' I said gently. 'Light passes out of a house, as well as in.'

'You mean . . . ?'

'I don't know. It isn't your business. Now steady up – Hagan's coming back with our glass.' The churning in my stomach was beginning to subside.

Hagan came into the yard carrying an oblong plastic-covered frame. I held the cheque out to him, but he was staring at Selina's face. He seemed to know immediately that our uncomprehending fingers had rummaged through his soul. Selina avoided his gaze. She was old and ill-looking and her eyes stared determinedly towards the nearing horizon.

'I'll take the rug from you, Mr Garland,' Hagan

finally said. 'You shouldn't have troubled yourself over it.'

'No trouble. Here's the cheque.'

'Thank you.' He was still looking at Selina with a strange kind of supplication. 'It's been a pleasure to do business with you.'

'The pleasure was mine,' I said in equal, senseless formality. I picked up the heavy frame and guided Selina towards the path which led to the road. Just as we reached the head of the now slippery steps Hagan spoke again.

'Mr Garland!'

I turned unwillingly.

'It wasn't my fault,' he said steadily. 'A hit-and-run driver got them both, down on the Oban road six years ago. My boy was only seven when it happened. I'm entitled to keep something.'

I nodded wordlessly and moved down the path, holding my wife close to me, treasuring the feel of her arms locked around me. At the bend I looked back through the rain and saw Hagan sitting with squared shoulders on the wall where we had first seen him.

He was looking at the house, but I was unable to tell if there was anyone at the window.

The first glimmer of light

The core idea for 'Light of Other Days' came in the most routine way possible. I was glancing through a school text-book on elementary physics – don't ask why – and happened to notice a paragraph on the phenomenon of a stick appearing to bend when it is put into water at an angle. The explanation was that light slows down a little when it is passing through water or glass.

One of the few facts that most people retain from their school days is that light travels at 186,000 miles a second. (If you went to school later than I did, the figure is more likely to be 300,000 kilometres a second, but it comes to the same thing.) No matter how little we can actually remember about the Wars of the Austrian Succession, or the Repeal of the Corn Laws, the retention of that precious number gives us a comforting feeling that our years of education have not been a total waste. Something we tend to forget, however, is that our science teachers were talking about the speed of light in *a vacuum*. It does indeed slow down a little when passing through a dense transparent medium, such as water; hence the apparent bending of the stick. (The detailed mechanics and optics of exactly how nature achieves this trick would occupy a hefty paragraph, and will not be dealt with here.)

What it all boils down to is that when you see an event through a pane of glass you see it a tiny fraction of a second later than you would have done had the glass not been there. That fact was far from new to me, but the Brownies in my sub-conscious must have been specially alert that day – and the bell of inspiration was rung.

What if, I thought, *somebody invented a type of glass which slowed light down by years instead of nanoseconds? If that happened, when you looked through a window you would see what had been on the other side years earlier!*

That's all there was to it. The idea was not remarkable or abstruse. It had been lying around for ages, available to anyone, ever since physicists began to understand the nature of light – but, as I said, my subconscious was really on form that day. All those shakings by the throat had encouraged it to start earning its keep.

Now for the hard part

The original idea was deceptively simple. Now that I consider the matter, it wasn't even *deceptively* simple – it was *simple*, and that was all there was to say on that point. It was time to begin plotting.

In spite of the simplicity, however, I could tell that I was on to something with lots of potential. The first plot I came up with dealt with the predicament of a judge in a murder case where there had been only one direct 'witness' to the crime – a piece of slow glass ten years thick. The judge is required to pass the death sentence, the accused is executed, and then the judge – who is prey to private doubts – has to wait almost ten years to see if he will be vindicated.

That was a good story in my opinion, but I decided to put it aside, feeling that it wasn't the most suitable vehicle for my idea's first venture into the public's awareness. A quest for the *right* plot had begun, and it went on for about two years, on and off. During that time I came up with plot after plot, any one of which would have made a saleable story, but I shelved them all, driven by a feeling that I was honour-bound to get as near to perfection as was possible for me.

Finally, I decided that it was the emotional value of slow glass that should be exploited, rather than any of its numerous technical aspects. The glass's ability to show what was on the other side years earlier directed me towards the emotion of nostalgia. I could go for the poignancy which can be felt when we are strongly reminded of times lost, things lost, *people* lost.

That decision led me fairly directly to the tormented Hagan, whose wife and child – although dead – could be seen every day at the window of his cottage. It would have been possible at that stage to write an unremittingly sad story with a downbeat ending, but there was a certain purity and beauty in the concept of slow glass which I deemed to be uplifting, and which should be represented in the plot. In any case, there was the writer's technical consideration that Hagan's unhappiness could be emphasised to the full by contrasting it with somebody else's joy. And what could be more satisfying from the author's point of view than having that joy brought about by the slow glass itself?

That was the thinking which brought the poet Garland and his wife Selina on to the scene as customers for a section of glass. They were deeply unhappy – but for selfish reasons – and by the end of the story they had come to realise just how lucky they actually were. To my mind, a kind of justice had been done, a balance achieved. One marriage had been cruelly terminated by an accident; another had been pre-served through circumstances directly resulting from the same accident.

Plotting as you go

As you will have noticed, I advocate a cerebral approach to plotting. That is the method which guarantees results, but much of the pleasure would be taken away from writing if it were possible to anticipate in full detail, and overcome every problem which crops up in the construction of a story. If the whole thing could be thought out in advance, down to the last nut and bolt and the last lick of paint, the actual writing would become a semi-mechanical process of merely fleshing out a skeleton.

This applies especially to the case of the novel, where it would be unreasonable to expect one's brain to accommo-date the entire scenario. In my early days as a writer, still unchastened by experience, I used to try doing exactly that – and found myself passing out in my favourite armchair through sheer mental overload! It's funny how writers often seek analogies when trying to describe problems peculiar to their own craft, but there is one which is appropriate to the job of plotting a novel. Anybody who has been employed to varnish the floor of a room should always contrive to finish at the door. The same general principle applies to plotting a story – cover the area thoroughly and make sure you can step out smartly at the end without making any unsightly disturbances which have to be worked over again.

We could use the terms strategic plotting – which is done before you begin to write; and tactical plotting – which takes place during the writing. 'Light of Other Days', being so short, did not require much of the latter, but there were a few points that needed attention. For example, because slow glass does not exist I felt the reader should be informed right from the outset that the story was set in the future. It had a contemporary *feel* to it, so it had to take place in the very near future, but you should be wary of specifying actual dates in cases like this. Time's winged chariot can overtake a story so quickly. Also, when you do pick out a date, perhaps only five years off, the reader may feel challenged to check out your thinking – sf fans have a leaning towards that kind of thing – and the illusory world of your story will develop a few cracks, not because the reader eventually agrees or disagrees with you – but because he has wandered out of your mental control. He has no business doing calculations – he should be comprehensively seduced, yielding to all your storytelling blandishments.

In the second paragraph of 'Light of Other Days', therefore, I mentioned that the 'car's turbine was pulling quietly and smoothly in the damp air'. Turbine engines for everyday road cars are a thing of the future, maybe not very far in the future, and so by inserting one into the narrative I had made the point.

Another example of tactical plotting was the decision to

make Garland a poet. The basic idea of slow glass seemed poetic to me, so there was a nice correspondence there, but I had other motives. And one of them was that I hadn't the foggiest notion of how slow glass might work! Science-fiction writers often find themselves in that predicament, and a good way of getting out of it is deliberately to make your viewpoint characters non-technical and non-scientific. The fact that I didn't know how slow glass worked did not stop me from going on to write more short stories about it, and eventually to incorporate them in a successful novel: *Other Days, Other Eyes*.

We are now reaching a grey area in which detailed plotting begins to merge with policy decisions about which kind of science fiction you should write – 'hard' or 'soft' – and that is the main subject of the next chapter.

4

'HARD' OR 'SOFT' SCIENCE FICTION?

As soon as you start to take a serious interest in writing science fiction, you will discover that experts divide it into two broad categories – 'hard' and 'soft'. This is a very neat arrangement, but it has a drawback in that nobody is entirely certain what the terms mean.

I bandied them around for years in the belief that the former dealt with hard disciplines such as electronics, astronomy and nuclear physics, while the latter was concerned with more humanist subjects like psychology, linguistics and sociology. That definition still stands for many people, but there is another school of thought which opines that hard sf is the type which has a good chance of coming true, while soft sf is the more fanciful variety which – while providing good entertainment – is a bit far-fetched.

For quite a long time I tried to accommodate both those beliefs, telling myself they amounted to roughly the same thing. After all, a story written by a man who was a tough-minded electronics engineer in real life was more likely to come to pass than one produced by somebody who dealt in abstracts most of the time and had never even set foot in a laboratory. Then it came to me that a writer such as Larry Niven, famous for some the hardest sf around, had built much of his reputation on novels like *Ringworld*, which have just about zero probability. At the same time J. G. Ballard, archetypal *soft* sf writer, was telling us that modern urban life was going to drive people completely insane – a prophecy which was coming true even as he was making it.

Confusing, isn't it?

It is important for the beginning sf writer to have some idea of which category his work may be lumped into – even if for no other reason than that the knowledge will give him some control of the situation. A versatile writer may decide in advance that his next story will be hard or soft, and in that way improve his marketing aim.

In reaching for a good working definition here, I can't do better than to quote Christopher Evans, who has said that 'hard' and 'soft' are 'loose terms which broadly separate writers who strive for a conspicuous show of scientific accuracy from those who are more concerned with social and metaphorical possibilities and never mind the nuts and bolts.'

One of the things which appeals to me about that quotation is the delicate cynicism, i.e. realism, which shades the words 'strive' and 'conspicuous'. Let's face it. If a person really knew how to build an anti-gravity machine he would be out there making billions from it – not sitting around the house writing stories. I'm not saying that the latter is a less laudable pursuit, but human nature raises its ugly head again . . .

The science of being scientific

The amazing, and comforting, thing about writing sf in the hard mode is that – properly done – it can persuade the reader that the author has the ability, in theory if not in practice, to turn his fictional devices into reality. Robert Silverberg is an American author who writes hard sf with the best in the world, but more than once I have heard him being driven into a corner by a fan who craved more and more detail about the workings of an imaginary machine, society or eco-system. Silverberg then puts on an expression of wry apology and says, 'We make it all up out of our heads, you know.'

In an earlier chapter I stressed the need for extensive reading of science fiction, but made no mention of boning up on actual science texts. That was because some people have a natural leaning towards science and have a fair idea of what is going on in its multitudinous branches, even when they have had little or no formal scientific education. Others have the opposite turn of mind and find it very difficult to retain much in the way of scientific knowledge.

If you are in the latter group there is hardly any point in trying to 'cram' on such a vast subject. Attempting to do so could even be harmful, producing feelings of inferiority or futility. As I said earlier, being a bit weak on science is no real barrier to becoming a successful sf writer – it simply calls for a knowledgeable (crafty or cunning, if you like) approach.

The above is not to say that you should eschew scientific matters. It is probably worth taking a journal like *New Scientist* which, although widely read by professional scientists, has a policy of ensuring that a goodly proportion of its content is accessible to laymen. The plan is to read the parts you are happy to deal with – allowing fragments to flutter down into the subconscious – and not bother too much about articles which seem baffling or boring. Watching television programmes like *Tomorrow's World* is also helpful. You'll never get a BSc in this way, and you're not trying to – but you can learn to be at ease in your metier, to stop feeling like a total outsider, and thus acquire a useful fluency.

Another thing I'm *not* saying is that you should never

do any concentrated research on a scientific/technological subject. If you have a good idea for a specific story which features, say, deep-sea life forms – and which in your judgement needs to be presented in the hard sf mode – then you must do your homework. Raid the public library, deprive it of all books relating to your new amour, and immerse (no pun intended) yourself in them for as long as you need.

A pleasing spin-off from this kind of excursion into the realms of genuine science is that you sometimes get more than you bargained for. Many years ago I wrote a novel, *Medusa's Children*, which had an undersea setting. I needed some really bizarre and unpleasant denizens of the deep, so I decided to read up on those which actually existed down there and kit them out with a few gruesome embellishments from my imagination. In the event, I had to *tone down* some of the unmitigated and devious submarine nastiness I learned about! Nature can be the supreme sf writer.

Let me buy you a lemonade

Even when, in the development of a specific story idea, you have narrowed your focus to a single branch or twig of science, you may sometimes realise there is simply too much ground to cover. A good thing to do then is to consult an expert.

This is standard practice with many sf writers and there is little need to fear being rebuffed by the person you approach. There are few intellectual pleasures to equal that of having someone come to you with a look of respect and ask your advice about something. Scientists and technologists are just as susceptible to it as the rest of us, so the needed information is usually freely and gladly given. (Only in the case of a heavy, major novel, where the expert is required to put in serious work and perhaps travel, would the question of paying out money arise – but that is leaping beyond the scope of this book.) The promise of a free copy of the eventual published work goes down very well, and as icing on the cake you can name a suitable character or scientific device after your adviser. My work is peppered with such eponyms.

As with everything else connected with becoming a writer, it is best to use a hard-headed, calculating, self-interested approach to the business of recruiting brainpower. If, when at a social gathering, you realise that somebody there knows all about carnivorous plants – and you feel you might some day want to do a story featuring them – then you should consciously befriend and cultivate that person. Show your interest in his speciality, get his name and phone number, add him to your 'collection'. There doesn't have to be any element of insincerity involved – friendships based on a mutual interest tend to last very well. And even if there is a teeny bit of artfulness on your part – what the heck! You're a serious writer, not a dabbler.

It is, of course, unlikely that a new writer will simply bump into all the experts he could wish for, but they can be contacted by a variety of means: through nearby universities and polytechnics, through the publishers of their books, or through editors of periodicals in which they have written.

The science-fiction writer is lucky in that the field boasts of a rare phenomenon: conventions. At these gatherings, writers, readers, editors, artists, literary agents, booksellers, scientists, publishers, actors and even critics mingle on amiable terms. A high proportion of attendees are genuinely learned in subjects of interest to science-fiction writers, and are very obliging about passing on their knowledge. As a professional writer I am able to charge the cost of convention weekends as a business expense, without cheating the

Inland Revenue – although my accounts do tend to refer to them as conferences, which somehow sounds more business-like. In all seriousness, though, without conventions my ability to function as a writer would be impaired.

Moderation in all things

Researching for a story can be slow and difficult sometimes, but on other occasions it seems to go with magical ease, with great chunks of information dropping into your lap, seemingly tailored for your needs. If you ever get a feeling of unholy glee over discovering that somebody else has done part of your work for you – watch out! This is a warning, a sign that you should proceed with caution.

It is in the nature of science-fiction stories that they quite often require the author to pass sizeable wads of technical information on to the reader. An author, especially a beginner, has a perfectly natural desire to prove to all and sundry that he has done his homework, but in his eagerness to show this he may start plonking the stuff down on the page in barely digestible lumps, the literary equivalent of suet balls in a soup.

In the sf world this sin is known as 'info dumping' and is something to be avoided because it irritates most readers and interferes with the all-precious illusion of the story. If at all possible the vital information should be broken down into convenient units and fed into the narrative at a measured pace. It pays to be methodical here – make a list of all the points you must get across, and tick them off as you proceed.

Also try to avoid making bald statements like 'Chemical X explodes on coming in contact with chemical Y'. The information can be imparted more entertainingly, and dis-

HOW TO WRITE SCIENCE FICTION

creetly, by having a character almost make the dangerous blunder and then being told off by somebody more knowledgeable. Even better, the character could actually cause an explosion and come to realise his mistake when part of the scenery disappears.

It may not always be possible to employ this technique, of course – especially in short stories where brevity has to be given due consideration – but ideally the reader should be unaware of being primed with selected items of information. I have used a very basic illustration to get the point across, but in a real story the facts to be implanted in the reader's mind are likely to be more complex, thus giving the writer more chance to exercise his ingenuity and subtlety.

It's not what you say, it's the way that you say it

A major figure in sf in the first half of this century was Hugo Gernsback. Born in Luxembourg, he emigrated to the USA in 1904 and became a radio designer, writer, editor and publisher of numerous pulp magazines. His first novel had the title of *Ralph 124C 41+*, the digital part of which may be read as 'one to foresee for one' – reflecting Gernsback's passion for (rotten puns aside) prediction of technological wonders.

His stories, and those of his followers, typically featured a 'man in the street' who somehow got projected into the future. This Ordinary Joe was there only as a sounding board for a highly knowledgeable guide who would escort him around a future city, explaining with great enthusiasm – and copious footnotes – all of its scientific marvels.

This gosh-wow! style of sf was all right in its day, but in the 1930s, there came one of the true giants of the genre – John W. Campbell – editor of the trail-blazing and seminal

70

magazine *Astounding Science Fiction*. Campbell has had an immeasurable influence on modern sf. As a gifted writer he was quick to see that a better way to excite the reader's sense of wonder – rather than bombarding him with superlatives and exclamation marks – was to treat future technological marvels in a casual, slightly off-hand manner, just as we do today with satellite television and organ transplants. He urged writers to produce sf stories which read as though they were future *mainstream* stories which had slipped back to us through a time fault.

That advice proved to be one of the cornerstones of all modern science fiction, and it is very valuable to the new writer, particularly when deciding to write in the hard or soft mode. For one thing, it allows him to adopt a tactic like the one I have already mentioned with regard to 'Light of Other Days'.

In that story I made the hero a poet largely because we do not expect poets to be technological wizards. Garland is a man who is baffled and bored by science; therefore he cannot be expected to take much of it in. In consequence, he makes a pretty poor job of explaining how slow glass works, but that is *his* fault – not Bob Shaw's! Poor old Shaw, the reader feels, consciously or unconsciously playing along with the game. He's hovering there in the background, his brain bursting with everything there is to know about the theory and manufacture of slow glass, but he isn't able to put it down on the page because, unfortunately, this Garland character is scientifically illiterate.

H. G. Wells, who single-handedly invented modern sf, even anticipated Campbell with this literary device. In one of his earliest short stories, 'The Argonauts of the Air' (1895), he had a shot at anticipating manned flight – and got everything totally wrong. Perhaps sensing that he was on shaky ground, he decided to steer clear of excessive detail by distancing himself from his rail-launched aircraft.

The story beings: 'One saw Monson's Flying Machine from the windows of the trains passing either along the South-Western main line or along the line between Wimbledon and Worcester Park . . .' You see, already there is a note of familiarity, if not tiredness, creeping in – the local rail services merit more wordage than the flying machine.

The four long opening paragraphs go on in the same vein: '. . . excursionists from Portsmouth and Southampton and the West . . . five years had passed since the growth of the colossal iron groves . . . Isle of Wight trippers felt their liberty to smile . . . morning trainload of season-ticket holders . . . weary excursionists returning exhausted . . . bilious child . . . growing neglect as the months went by . . . money trickled away . . .'

The above is only a sample of the phrases which Wells concentrated into those paragraphs to produce, with superb effect, a mood of suburban *ennui*, of something being rusty, dusty and utterly commonplace. The flying machine and its ramp have begun to feel like the local gasometer – therefore, 'for the sake of the reader', the author has chosen not to go into too much descriptive detail.

That is clever and sophisticated sf writing – but not simply because it excused Wells, who qualified as a biologist, from having to flounder in the then ill-understood science of aerodynamics. The sheer novelty of a flying machine to the reader of 1895 must have been enormously enhanced by the notion of such a thing ever becoming a routine feature of daily life.

My admiration for Wells knows no bounds, all the more so because he proved himself human by making the occasional misjudgement. In 'The Land Ironclads' (1903), he predicted the use of tanks on the battlefield, and decided – probably because he was extrapolating contemporary technology only a little – to go in for our old friend, the 'conspicuous show of scientific accuracy'.

72

In that story the tanks were seen as a brand-new development, an emergent marvel, and therefore they had to be described in detail – but to anyone who knows anything about gunnery or automotive engineering, the long and particularised passages on how the juggernauts actually functioned are quite ludicrous. The lesson for us ordinary mortals is to resist any temptation to pretend that we can predict the future.

Isn't it marvellous how it all came true?

But surely, you could object, one of science fiction's chief claims to legitimacy is that it tells us the shape of things to come. Is that not what hard sf is all about?

Er, well, yes . . .

It is true that people who know very little about sf are convinced that its writers should be respected for their prophetic works. The sad fact, however, is that science fiction has a terrible record in this matter of prediction. It has always been the practice of sf writers to use the shotgun or scattergun technique when devising future scenarios. In other words, if you predict *everything*, now and then *something* will come true. It's a bit like horse racing. If you back every horse in a race you are bound to pick the winner, but it's nothing to boast about.

Science-fiction writers have the same weaknesses as the rest of the human race, so when we are being pressed by eager reporters – and the dreaded term 'sci-fi' keeps pounding on our ears – we often succumb to temptation and trot out some of the old fireside stories. A favourite is the one about the American writer, Cleve Cartmill, who in 1944 published a short story called 'Deadline', which dealt with nuclear warfare and in which Cartmill put forward his ideas on how to build an atomic bomb.

The day after the story was published the FBI descended and dragged him off to the clink. Their assumption seemed to be that he had penetrated the Manhattan Project and, instead of selling the intelligence to a foreign power for a vast sum, had decided to pass it on to his favourite science-fiction magazine for a cent per word. It took Cartmill a day or two to make the FBI understand that every physicist in the world knew in theory how to set off an atomic explosion. (The real difficulty was the practical one of assembling the refined materials in sufficient quantity, and from then on the most urgent problem was how to *stop* oneself from setting off an atomic explosion.)

There are some other examples. The helicopter pioneer Sikorsky is said to have been inspired by Jules Verne, and Arthur C. Clarke is noted for having conceived the idea of communications satellites and worked out their exact orbits, also in 1944. But in general sf writers got it all wrong – especially in their chosen territory of space exploration. In the great mid-century flowering of modern sf, for instance, it was generally agreed that by the 1990s Earth would be part of a tri-planetary empire, in association with Mars and Venus. Other roles were to be played by hardy colonists in the twilight zone of Mercury; by rough-and-tough miners in the asteroid belt between the orbits of Mars and Jupiter; and by futuristic Davy Crocketts on the moons of Jupiter and Saturn. It was all a Never-Never Land, of course, progressively banished from reality as the cold-eyed space probes began to spiral out from Earth.

When I was young the layout of that cosy solar system was more familiar to me, and more dear, than the geography of my native Northern Ireland. I have gone into the matter in some detail, not as an exercise in nostalgia, but because it is important for the beginning sf writer to realise that he cannot predict the future, and that he shouldn't hobble himself by trying.

The future is what you make it

Life would be terribly dull if we knew in advance what was going to happen to us; therefore we can take some comfort in the sheer cussedness of reality as it goes on confounding the most serious and best qualified futurologists. After all, if any sf writer had predicted that communism would expire within the space of a few months his vision would have been dismissed as purest fantasy.

It is in the very nature of things that problems can be anticipated well in advance of their solutions. That is why near-future scenarios drawn up in establishment think tanks tend to be depressing in the extreme. There is nothing standing in the way of a writer who has a good idea for a sombre, downbeat story based on current trends – but the range of possibilities is curtailed.

Brian Stableford, a prominent British sf writer with a gift for analysis, has made pertinent comments: '. . . the sf writer's quest is not for the most *likely*, but for the most *interesting* future. Careful and sensible extrapolation can easily result in stories which the readers will find dull.'

The message is not to play too safe. Giving your imagination full rein is likely to result in a more enjoyable story, which does not mean that it will be easier to write. The farther you go into the realms of the imagination, the harder you will have to work to maintain plausibility; but that is part of the fun of writing science fiction. One of the basic rules is to play up the plausibilities and play down the impossibilities – and this brings us to the interesting topic of the Secret Game.

Officially, one of the principal demarcations between fantasy and science fiction is that the events in the latter can have a scientific explanation, but players of the Secret Game have a sophisticated way of looking at these matters. (These players, by the way, are experienced sf writers and readers.)

Consider the basic example of space travel. Einstein's work on relativity has made all of us aware that nothing can travel faster than light. Even if a ship got very close to the speed of light it would take it more than four years to reach the nearest star – a fact which, to say the least of it, is a serious potential threat for the sf writer wrestling with his latest plot. This subject of FTL (faster-than-light travel) is so important that I will treat it at length in a later chapter, but for the moment let us deal with the fact that we are discussing impossibilities.

Science fiction is essentially *fiction* and nobody in his right mind ever forgets that. (Readers of the genre tend to be far more sceptical than the general public about UFO phenomena, ley lines, Atlantis, etc.) The basis of the Secret Game is that we all love a good story, and for that reason are prepared to make certain concessions when it comes to strict scientific accuracy. What the sf reader is *not* prepared to do is to throw scientific laws overboard without an acknowledgement that they existed in the first place.

He will accept a violation of the known laws of physics, but the rules of the game demand an indication that the author is perfectly aware of what he is doing. Nothing annoys the experienced reader more than (a) a conviction that the author can't recognise a scientific howler; (b) a suspicion that the author can spot it but thinks the reader *can't*; and (c) a feeling that the author believes it doesn't matter a damn anyway.

The sf reader is a quite reasonable person, generous by instinct, and you don't have to break your back to earn his cooperation in this respect. Sometimes a sentence, a phrase or even a single word – such as 'warp' – is enough to do the trick. As far as I know, it is impossible at present to build a workable helicopter which operates on battery power, but if you *need* one for a story you can deal with the problem by inserting a sentence which begins: 'Thanks to Hiyushi's great breakthrough in battery design in 1998 . . .'

What you are doing is tipping the reader a wink which says: 'Look, we both know that I'm bending the rules here, but if we allow pedantry to rule we're going to lose out on a good story.'

Scientists are often portrayed, especially on the screen, as rigid-minded types whose thinking is easily outpaced by that of the receptive young hero and heroine. In real life, though, I have found that scientists are more ready than most people to unleash their imaginations and take part in the game of 'What if . . . ?'. Science-fiction readers are cast in the same mould.

As I said, it's a kind of a game – but one whose rules should be taken seriously by the sf writer.

Would you believe it?

Whether or not you are going to write a story in the hard or soft mode, it is important not to make your chosen future *too* interesting. The writer aims to induce in the reader the famous 'willing suspension of disbelief' – and one way to spoil the mood is to pile on too much in the way of global menaces, wonderful inventions, and so on. There is a general rule that the reader should be asked to accept only one major novelty per story. It doesn't matter too much how fantastic or improbable it may be – the sf reader is a good sport in this matter, and he is willing to go along with your startling new premise, but only with one.

Suppose, for example, that you have an idea about a warfare chemist who is feckless enough to invent a nerve gas which is so powerful that one container of it is enough to kill everybody in the world. That's it! That is your one major novelty, and you are not allowed any more. You can have the container spring a leak, and you can have humanity starting to die off as the deadly molecules spread through the atmosphere. That is all right with the reader because those developments are a rational extension of your original concept. You could even have the chemist, who knows the gas better than anybody else, devise an antidote just in time to save a small group of people. (I don't need to remind you at this stage to leave it at that, and not have any characters called Adam and Eve lurking about.)

What you *cannot* do, however, is have the Earth suddenly pass through a vast interplanetary gas cloud which causes life-saving chemicals to filter down through the atmosphere. That would be major novelty Number Two – and the reader simply will not stand for it. If there is one Latin phrase that the sf fan knows by heart, and is prepared to use with withering effect, it is *deus ex machina*, meaning a specious and contrived ending, the literary pulling of a rabbit out of a hat.

For a bit of mental exercise, consider the following plot: the Earth's vegetable kingdom has been invaded by tall mobile plants whose whiplike sting is fatal to humans. As the plants can move only very slowly they don't pose much of a threat to anybody. Then there comes a strange meteor shower which causes nearly everybody in the world to go blind. All at once the plants are a *terrible* danger, because blind people keep blundering into them, and the human race has one hell of a job to survive.

Familiar? Yes, we're looking at John Wyndham's famous *Day of the Triffids*, published in 1951. I hate clichés, but this is one of the exceptions which proves the rule. As is obvious, Wyndham broke the single-novelty rule and got away with it, but the story remains flawed and tends to be more popular with the casual reader than with aficionados. Yes, yes, I *know* we would all like to produce 'failures' which get made into major films, but the sf world today is very different from what it was in 1951.

Writing is more of an art than a craft; therefore it is possible for the accomplished author, when the notion takes him, to thumb his nose at every rule ever invented. But for the beginning sf writer it is highly advisable to pay attention to all the conventions, and to learn to deal with them before beginning to flex his literary muscles.

5

CHARACTERISATION

One of the charges often laid against science fiction is that it has no characterisation worthy of the name.

There is no point in denying the charge. Thousands upon thousands of sf stories have been peopled by nothing more than the proverbial cardboard cutouts; and even greater numbers have featured what might be described as tissue-paper cutouts. In these yarns the characterisation is so nominal as to be practically non-existent.

'Great!' you may cry. 'I will fill *my* stories with genuine, rounded, fully realised, flesh-and-blood characters. My characterisation will be as good as in any mainstream fiction. It will be something to which sf readers are unaccustomed, and I will be able to take the field by storm.'

That is a perfectly natural, and laudable, reaction – but at this point, a word of warning! As is so often the case in the writing of sf, things are not as simple and as cut and dried as they may seem.

Knowing where to stop

One thing you have to consider is the likelihood that most science-fiction devotees *have* previously been exposed to good characterisation – during their reading of mainstream books and magazines. (The science-fiction field is noted for its high proportion of fanatical followers, but these tend also to have read widely in other categories.) It is even possible that many of them deserted the mainstream precisely because they became impatient with penetrating character studies and wanted to enjoy, say, puzzle stories in which the fictional problems were laid out for them as succinctly as possible.

Science fiction, by its very nature, is suited to puzzle stories. They are an integral and respected part of the field, and the reader would probably be justified in complaining about an example which was plumped up with a lot of characterisation. It would get in the way of the story's legitimate aims. Boiling the matter down to the absurd, the old joke about the man who dreamed he was eating peppermints, and woke up to find the buttons gone from his pyjamas, would not be improved by the addition of 5,000 words detailing the traumas of his past life.

We are, despite jokey references, touching on serious issues here.

Many writers deplore the categorisation of fiction – claiming it is an artificial device forced on them by booksellers – but it is a fact of life and there is no use pretending that it isn't. In some respects I would prefer a literary climate such as existed at the turn of the century, in which even the most eminent writers would occasionally turn their hands to what we now classify as science fiction, and the stories were published in mainstream journals without a word of discriminatory editorial comment. On the other hand, the mustard-keen fan of sf (or any other category) appreciates not having to spend time searching through irrelevant material.

The point is that, when you are sitting down to write a science-fiction story, it is worth bearing in mind that readers – and editors! – may not *want* a great deal of wordage devoted to characterisation. This is not pure philistinism; rather, it is a recognition of the fact that a piece of science fiction usually has to accommodate a range of 'characters' which are rare in the mainstream. The *idea* can assume the role of a character, as can other elements such as an *alien environment* or an *alien society*. There is a limit to how much even the most skilled writer can cram into a few hundred pages, and this is one of the reasons the sf field abounds in trilogies and series. (A popular in-joke among authors is the reference to working on the 'sixth book of my trilogy'.)

It's all part of what we have already referred to as the 'distinctiveness' of science fiction – the necessity for a sf story to provide something which is not available in any other branch of literature.

Trying to fight City Hall

Early in my career I fell into the trap of deciding to write a novel in which the action, settings and – above all – characters would be handled exactly as in a decent mainstream book. I set to with great enthusiasm and produced *The Ground Zero Man* – a novel, set in near-future England, about the awful trouble a scientist gets into when he creates a machine which can explode every nuclear bomb in the world at the same time. When the MS was duly mailed off to my usual publisher, via my literary agent, I sat back with a self-satisfied smirk and waited for the adulation.

What actually happened was that my agent got a rather terse letter turning the book down. Adding what I saw as insult to injury, the letter concluded by saying: 'We have an option on Bob Shaw's next science-fiction novel – and as *The Ground Zero Man* can by no stretch of the imagination be described as science fiction – that option is unaffected and remains in force.'

The book *was* eventually brought out by that self-same publisher, quite a few years later and under a different editor, but the episode poses an intriguing question. How could a story which is set in the future and concerns a fictional scientist and a fictional scientific device fail to be classed as science fiction? The answer is that it didn't have the *feel* of science fiction. I had failed to give the idea its due prominence as a character. I stoutly maintain that my treatment of the story was superior to the accepted sf treatment of the day. It has recently been reprinted with some updating as *The Peace Machine*, and, significantly, has led to many people asking me why I never became a thriller writer.

But, and it is a big *but*, although I personally saw the book as an artistic success, it came near to being a total failure in terms of my main objective – which was to make sure that everything I wrote reached the maximum possible audience, with a commensurate financial reward. The moral is that if you want to succeed in sf it is advisable to pay attention to the genre's ground rules.

A friend of mine once summed the matter up by saying: 'Why should I turn to science fiction for character studies when I still haven't read all of Dostoevsky?'

I'm not trying to give the impression that characterisation has no place in a science-fiction story. Far from it! A science-fiction story should have the exact amount and type of characterisation that it needs – and the author has to be able to make an informed judgement as to how much this should be.

All right, how do you go about it?

Characters in context

The obvious method is that of compression, the telling detail which conveys a wealth of information. The snag is this method usually does not travel well from the mainstream to the specialised world of science fiction. A mundane author may write: 'Forsythe-Williams adjusted his monocle', or 'Joe Bloggs splashed tomato ketchup on his chips'. In each case the author, by expending only a few words, has drawn upon the equivalent of *millions* of words represented by the reader's familiarity with his own society. Even the characters' names speak volumes!

By contrast, look at what happens when a science-fiction writer tries the same trick, the same shorthand. He may write: 'Nargle ordered a glass of glymm juice'. The sentence looks much the same as the two previous examples, but how much background information does it convey? None! The reader doesn't know if 'Nargle' is a patrician or a plebeian name. He doesn't know if glymm juice is on a par with champagne or brown ale. For all he knows, a member of the imaginary society orders a drink in a glass – in preference to one in a ceramic mug – only when he wants to be safe against poisoning, or to celebrate the shedding of his third skin, or to challenge his neighbour to a duel.

The possibilities multiply endlessly, and the closer they get to infinity the more work the sf writer is called upon to do to bring the unruly herd of variables under his personal control.

This book deals with the special concerns of science-fiction writers, so I am not going to devote a lot of space to the general principles and techniques of characterisation which can readily be gleaned from other sources. The main thing is for the beginning sf writer to go into the arena with his eyes wide open; to be fully aware of the unique problems; and, on the positive side, to be *stimulated* by the difficulties so that, instead of perhaps handling characteris-ation in a perfunctory manner, he is inspired to draw upon unknown creative reserves.

So far in this chapter I have been emphasising the diffi-culties of characterisation in sf, but there are also many favourable winds and tides.

Human characters

When it comes to characterisation, one of the most basic and influential things an author can do is to describe the appearance of his fictional personalities. I would imagine – though I might be challenged on this – that even a blind person reading in Braille would value these summaries of visual characteristics, if only as a means of keeping tabs on the various players as they step out of the narrative limelight and reappear perhaps many pages later.

In science fiction, because of its limitless possibilities, the author has the opportunity to go on descriptive binges. But beware of the temptation to overindulge at the banquet; and, in particular, be careful about allure of characterisation by quirk. In sf it is easy to create a seven-foot-tall albino Eskimo who has lost one eye and in its place wears an egg-sized opal; who is minus one of his hands and instead has been provided with a cluster of multi-connectors which enable him to plug into and control any machine in the universe; and who flits around in an antigravity sled which emits purple smoke.

Such exterior adornments are all very well, but the reader will not become involved with your character unless he is induced to sympathise with him and pray for his success; or – something equally effective – to be persuaded to hate the character and pray for him to get his comeuppance.

It is generally inadvisable, therefore, to spend a *lot* of wordage on the physical description of any character. For most purposes, a paragraph is enough the first time a character appears, and the description should be done as clearly as possible. Try to *see* your invented person – if necessary going as far as making a sketch – and then try to make the reader see him as well.

In that introductory paragraph you will possibly mention as many as six or eight graphic details, depending on your own style and inclinations. The character may go off-stage for quite long periods, and each time he comes back into the focus of the narrative it is worth reminding the reader who he is. (The name alone is not enough, even for major characters. How many times have you been reading a novel, and a third of the way into it had a name spring off the page at you, forcing you to turn back to the beginning to find out if he is the hero or merely some auxiliary?)

Obviously, you don't want to repeat the character's physical description in its entirety, so it is a good idea – while penning that initial paragraph – to select one salient feature and earmark it for use as the character's motif. Every time he pops up again you should sound that key note in a few words, with variations of course. In this way it is possible to reinforce the reader's memory, and greatly increase his involvement in and enjoyment of your story, with a highly satisfying economy of words.

In science fiction there is the chance to strengthen the fabric of a story by linking characters' personal appearance to their environment. A human settler who has grown up on a low-gravity world can be expected to be much taller than a person from Earth; similarly, one who comes from a planet with a sparse atmosphere will have a very large chest capacity. If you bring these characters to Earth they will suffer various kinds of discomfort, unless special provisions have been made in a reception centre or the Galactic

Hilton. Conversely, if you send ordinary humans into the settlers' environment, the fictional tables will be turned.

Alien characters

Possibly the most constructive thing you can do when it comes to characterising an alien being is to admit – right from the outset – that the task is impossible.

This is being realistic rather than defeatist, and there is no need to feel guilty about it. Consider, for example, the situation you would be in if you had only two characters in a story: a man, and a cobra.

You could no doubt acquit yourself well if you were required to produce an archetypal *Wide World* adventure in which the intrepid adventurer has to get past the snake and out of the cave before he faints from the pain in his broken leg. *But*, what if the imposition was to produce a story in which the explorer and the cobra become friends, have long conversations, and go off together to overthrow a local tyrant?

Obviously, such a fiction could not be created on any kind of realistic level, even though, compared to an interstellar alien, the cobra has to be as familiar and as endearing to us as Aunt Mabel's pet spaniel. The cobra was spawned from our common ancestral primordial soup, it has shared the planet with us for millions of years, and yet as far as we are concerned it is an alien creature; what, then, would we think about a life form which originated on a different kind of planet, orbiting a different kind of sun in a distant galaxy? Logically, such a creature is bound to be far more alien than our dear old cousin, the homely cobra. It is bound to be alien to the nth degree – and totally beyond human comprehension. It could be argued that the gulf between man and snake is largely created by the fact that one is intelligent and one isn't; but it is likely that, were the snake to be given some tens of millions of years to develop its IQ, it would become even *more* snaky, even *more* alien, even *more* incomprehensible.

Where does that leave you, after having rashly committed yourself to populating part of a manuscript with aliens? Oddly enough, if you keep a level head you can do rather well out of the situation. You can even capitalise on the difficulties – and this is part of the sheer enjoyment and challenge of writing science fiction.

How alien can you get?

The first step is to slot your alien into one of two basic categories: 'opaque' or 'translucent'.

The labels should be self-explanatory, but just to sum up: an opaque alien is akin to the cobra; a translucent alien is more akin to Aunt Mabel's spaniel, or perhaps to Aunt Mabel herself.

When you create an opaque alien you are being a realist and admitting that nobody can have insight with regard to such a creature. Its very impenetrability can then be turned to your advantage, because you are required to deal only with its externals, to report on its appearance and actions. This distancing of the subject is in accord with the situation which would prevail if you really did see a spaceship disgorging large beings with the wrong number of legs. (This is something of an aside, but there is nothing like giving a creature a multiplicity of legs to make the reader highly wary of it and uncomfortable in its presence. The fear of spiders is so strong and universal – I have dubbed it the 'arachnid reaction' – that there are some grounds for believing they did not originate on this planet. We all know that two is the right number of legs to have; we can accept four quite well, largely because of adorable ponies and Aunt Mabel's pet spaniel; six is definitely getting beyond the joke, even though the humble bluebottle has been around for ever; but when it gets to *eight* . . . !)

Opaque aliens cannot be *characterised*, but they can be *individualised* by the trick mentioned earlier in this chapter: relating appearance to home environment. One of my first novels, *The Palace of Eternity*, featured some highly satisfactory nasties called Syccans. They came to Earth from a planet of endless rain; therefore they needed water continually falling on their skins, and therefore, whenever they were on Earth, like humans needing oxygen tanks on Mars, they wore devices which showered them with water.

That worked out pretty well – nice bit of exotic detail – but the Syccans had to be *really* loathsome, so I went a bit further into their environmental background and came up with the notion that, as they would never need to wash, their outlook on personal hygiene could be a lot different from ours. Where did that get me? Well, here are three of them in action . . .

The mist from the overhead nozzles attached to the tanks on their backs billowed over everything in the room, filling it with a foetid humidity, condensing on and lubricating the exposed, palpitating lungs and other organs of the aliens. Mewing and clicking sounds came from their shoulder-mouths . . . A valve in the central alien's lower gut popped loudly, spattering the other two with grey-and-white excrement which was gradually washed away by their sprays, and the silence resumed . . .

Fairly disgusting, I admit, but it made for damned good

aliens. I have been complimented many times on my Syccans, and accept the praise with glee because – and I make no apology for reiterating this – writing sf has to be approached with zest. Address yourself to humanity's weightiest problems, by all means, but at the same time make use of all the recreational possibilities. Designing a really good monster can be fun!

Moving on to translucent aliens, you should accept that as soon as you presume to see some distance into them they will cease to *be* aliens. Any character you give them will be a reflection of some part of your own human character – even when you deliberately invert the reflection. Again, this is not an occasion for despair. One of the quickest roads to success in any branch of the arts or crafts is to learn the best methods of cheating – and successfully portraying the translucent alien is a sub-division of sf which *demands* sophisticated and knowledgeable cheating. Your aliens may be humans in disguise, but if you use imagination and ingenuity to make their disguise a clever one, you will have fulfilled your contract with the reader. After all, the object of writing science *fiction* is not to design 'real' extraterrestrials, any more than the object of writing fairy stories is to anatomise Tinkerbell.

You're just being contrary

Inversion, mentioned above, is an effective technique which involves taking basic human attitudes or attributes and standing them on their head. For example, no man or woman in good mental and physical health wants to die. The prospect is so abhorrent that for the most part we avoid even thinking about it – therefore, an alien character who didn't mind dying, and perhaps even looked forward to it, would be alien in the extreme.

One of the best treatments of this idea was in Hal Clement's novel *Cycle of Fire*. The baffled anguish of the human protagonist, as he fails in all his attempts to talk his alien friend into seeing 'reason' and going on living, has lingered in my memory for decades. Another early example cropped up in Stanley G. Weinbaum's 1934 short story 'The Lotus Eaters', in which a human explorer on Mars discovers an intelligent vegetable. He is having a philosophical chat with the vegetable when, to his horror, he notices that it is being devoured by an animal and will soon be all gone. The point of the story, which was well ahead of its time, was that the vegetable – not being prey to human emotions – was not at all bothered about being eaten and calmly went on philosophising until the last possible moment. I read that story about forty years ago, and today I sometimes become irritated with myself for letting such a naive, immature and obvious example of inversion stick in my mind. But it *worked*, dammit!

Just about anything is possible in sf, so another highly successful way of dealing with alien characters is cheerfully to abandon the attempt to portray them as anything other than humans in disguise. That approach, which lends itself to lightweight stories, was pioneered by Eric Frank Russell, the Cheshire-based writer who almost single-handedly invented the cute, lovable alien. Lines such as 'Captain Grekle twitched his third pseudopod – the Arcturian equivalent of looking embarrassed', were EFR's trademark and have been made good use of by later generations of writers.

One of the nagging problems in dealing with translucent aliens is that of communication. Opaque aliens are no bother in this respect – they don't talk to us, and we don't talk to them – but once you start to characterise aliens there pretty well has to be some kind of dialogue. The writer's options are limited here, and none of them is entirely satis-factory – so it is a good idea to weigh up the various draw-backs before you sit down at the keyboard.

We have already admitted that our aliens will be humans in disguise, but it is a flimsy disguise indeed if they speak fluent English and can handle the subjunctive like an Oxbridge don. Perhaps the most naturalistic and sensible thing to do is have both parties get together and conduct language courses. The snag, as far as drama is concerned, is that the process could take years and could not readily be accommodated in most plots. Anyway, an alien who agreed to do that would be behaving in a more human manner than most humans.

Another old standby is: 'We learned your language and customs by studying television transmissions which leaked into space'. I suppose that is a *kind* of rationalisation, but the distorted impression an alien would get of our lan-guage(s) and culture(s) by studying a jumble of TV pro-grammes from afar is a fit subject for satire.

Then there is the universal translator – a wonderfully versatile device, quite often worn near the throat, which enables space travellers to engage in immediate conver-sation, no matter how disparate their backgrounds. In spite of its sheer impossibility, both in theory and practice, the universal translator keeps popping up in one form or another because writers find it so useful. However, the incredible pace of development in microcomputers permits us to look at the idea of a *smart* universal translator. The SUT might deduce what an alien is saying from circumstance and context, starting off with an understanding of only two or three sounds and rapidly building a useful vocabulary. There are opportunities here for some clever writing, especially for those with the relevant technical or scientific qualifications, but don't try it unless you have definitely made up your mind to write hard science fiction.

Finally, in this section, there is our old friend: telepathy.

I don't know what science fiction, science fantasy, fantasy, supernatural, horror, and imaginative writing in general would have done if the human race had not clutched the notion of telepathy to its collective bosom a long time ago. There is not a shred of scientific evidence to suggest that the faculty exists, even in the most rudimentary form, but somehow the idea of unassisted mind-to-mind communication at a distance is so beguiling that we simply refuse to give it up.

If telepathy between humans is impossible, then, logically, telepathy between humans and aliens should be even more of a non-starter. Many times when doing the initial plotting for a story I have sworn a mighty vow not to fall back on such a hoary and unlikely device once my humans meet up with my translucent aliens. Hah! After a few hours of torturing my brain, I have always undergone an almost religious conversion, becoming more liberal and tolerant in my outlook.

Who am I to decide what fantastic mental powers an advanced creature from another planet might have? is the way my thinking usually goes on such occasions.

Telepathy is destined to remain as a major avenue of communication between humans and aliens in sf, simply because the authors can hardly do without it. As is so often the case in this kind of writing, an intelligent appreciation of the difficulties should stimulate you to devise ingenious ways around them. And by making the reader aware of unanticipated problems, and then ostentatiously solving them, you can give your writing an extra air of authority.

Exotic names

Names are an important part of characterisation in any branch of fiction. Their role is enhanced in sf, but beware of going over the top.

When one is deciding what an extraterrestrial should be called, there is a powerful temptation to suggest its alien origins by, for instance, giving it a name which contains no vowels. That trick has been worked close to death over the decades, and there is the risk of producing something which is unintentionally ridiculous or which irritates the reader. Although we don't move our lips when reading, we expect words to be pronounceable. It is also advisable to avoid names which end in 's' – otherwise there can be awkwardness with the possessive.

Another pitfall to be wary of is the use of typographical quirks. They may feel clever, they may look clever, but the result is a distraction from the narrative. One of the first science-fiction short stories I ever read featured an alien which introduced itself to some humans as 'iGlann'.

'Gosh, that's really *alien*!' I exclaimed, my adolescent mind deeply impressed. It was not until days later that I began to have niggling worries about how the humans *knew* the first letter in the alien's name was in lower case and the second in upper.

That objection to 'iGlann' may seem pernickety in the extreme, but nevertheless it had lodged itself in my subconscious and was surreptitiously undermining the foundations of the story. The lesson is that you should never be perfunctory or superficial about any aspect of a story, especially characterisation. By enjoying the challenge and getting everything as right as possible, down to the last microscopic detail, you can go a long way towards one of the science-fiction writer's principal goals – persuading the reader to suspend disbelief.

6

DO-IT-YOURSELF PLANETS

I am no great admirer of science fiction on the screen. To me it is sad that the genre's crowning glory, its wealth of ideas – subtle or startling, poignant or comic – is ignored by makers of space pantomimes whose all-important monetary success depends on graphic violence and special effects.

Having said that, however, there are some facets of the science-fiction diamond which the cinema can display superbly. One of them is that exquisite moment when a spaceship lands on a far-distant planet. The sound of the engines dies away . . . hydraulics start to whine . . . the door beings to open . . . the first tantalising glimpses of an alien landscape are revealed . . . the astronauts crane forward . . .

At that moment, I too am craning forward, and the single thought on my mind – because I'm in tune with the fictional space travellers – is: What am I going to see? *What am I going to see*?

That craving to gorge one's eyes on something genuinely and utterly new is a chief characteristic of the human race, and it lies behind men like Columbus and Cook setting off on their famous voyages. It should be realised that their expeditions represented a much greater penetration of the *unknown* than the fairly recent flights to the Moon. Initially they had *no* inkling of what lay ahead, they had *no* guarantee whatsoever of being able to return – but they went because they simply had to see what was out there.

Science-fiction enthusiasts either share that yearning or empathise with it. Although they can't stand beside Cortez on that peak in Darien, with looks of 'wild surmise', they love to do the next-best thing – which is to first-foot imaginary new worlds. The cinema has an initial advantage over print in this respect, because the first few seconds of the experience are predominantly visual, but the writer soon comes into his own – especially if he has served his apprenticeship in the craft of building planets.

Background or foreground?

In an earlier chapter we dealt with the technique of using a matter-of-fact approach to our fictional wonders to increase their impact on the reader's mind. But that mainly referred to the scientific marvels of a future human society. When you inveigle the reader to join you on an exotic alien world you are perfectly entitled to convey your own awe at what is being unfolded 'before your very eyes', and to use all your descriptive ability to excite his sense of wonder. In fact, you are pretty well *required* to do so – otherwise, what is the point in taking him there in the first place?

There are, however, a few relevant points to consider.

If the exotic locale is there principally as a colourful background for a sequence of events there is no need to spend a lot of time on astronomical, geological and other scientific underpinnings. The environment should have coherence, but the reader is not going to fret much if, for example, he suspects that your sunsets are too splendid for a world with a dust-free and unpolluted atmosphere.

On the other hand, if your story is set on an invented

world because some unique feature of that world is vital to the plot, then it is advisable to do adequate groundwork. If you don't make the planet believable and give it a feeling of solidity, the related part of the story will be robbed of the precious sense of inevitability. The reader won't feel that things happened in a certain way because they *had* to happen that way, and once he decides you are trumping things up, you have probably lost him. He may be persuaded to stick around for a while to admire your ingenuity, but it would be better for all concerned if he kept on reading because he had no conscious choice in the matter.

Designing an entire planet may sound like a superhuman undertaking, perhaps even vaguely sacrilegious, but it can be done in a series of small and logical steps. And of course you are not required to draw up a complete specification – you have only to meet the artistic needs of your story. In fact, there can be a danger, mentioned earlier, of having too much lovely, juicy research data at your disposal, and deciding it would be a shame to let it go to waste.

Each and every bit of information that the reader is entitled to should be presented to him scrupulously, but beware of info dumping, otherwise known in the trade as the 'expository lump'. Some authors are good at mathematics and celestial mechanics, and – especially the ones who are fond of computers – enjoy producing reams upon reams of pertinent technical data before beginning work on a story. The theory is that the reader, even if he is not consciously aware of all the meticulous substructuring, will intuit that it has been done and will feel increased respect for the author and the story. That's fine within reasonable limits – the groundwork has to be done – but I suspect that much of the reason for the copious printouts is that the authors are having fun. Nobody is going to convince me that someone, having just read an intriguing, exciting, superbly plotted, well-characterised, beautifully written sf story, has ever set it down and said, 'I suppose that *might* have been a decent enough yarn if the author hadn't spoiled everything by getting the longitude of the planet's perihelion wrong.'

Step by step

There was a time when sf writers didn't have much need to go in for planet building. That was because we had a menu of interesting worlds on our own astronomical doorstep, ready-made settings for adventure. Mars was believed to have canals and an adequate if somewhat skimpy atmosphere. There were taverns in the green strips along the canals, where spacemen drank and brawled at night while the tiny twin moons raced overhead, and out in the desert the ruins of the Old Civilisation brooded on the past aeons. Improved telescopes and then space probes deprived us of all that.

Venus was even better value for sf writers because, being completely covered by cloud, it came in two varieties – swamp world absolutely swarming with exotic life forms, or Sahara-like world with a reasonable selection of exotic life forms. Even Mercury was a usable locale in spite of being so close to the Sun, because it was thought to have a twilight zone in which astronauts could survive without too much trouble.

It all turned out to be hopelessly inaccurate. With the advance of science in this century writers were driven off our local worlds altogether, or had their activities severely curtailed. It is still possible to use the Moon or Mars as settings, but we now know so much about them that the stories would have to be hard sf at its hardest. Besides that, the dramatic possibilities are limited – there is only so much one can do with a handful of characters who spend all their time in spacesuits or pressure domes.

One trick the sf writer can employ is to bring in the science of 'terraforming', the use of super-engineering to modify entire planets to suit the needs of humans. This notion has engendered many good stories, but by definition it is the opposite of creating viable *alien* planets.

The above considerations are what have encouraged modern sf writers to strike out into the wild black yonder when their imaginations need a bit of elbow room. There are at least a hundred billion stars in our galaxy, and there are at least a hundred billion galaxies in the universe – so, even if only a tiny fraction of stars have a retinue of planets, there is an unimaginable number of alien worlds out there. But that very profusion of possibilities imposes on the writer an obligation to exercise self-restraint.

W. S. Gilbert said, 'Where everybody is somebody, nobody is anybody.' Translated into science-fiction terms, that means, 'Where *anything* is possible, nothing is wonderful.'

That, basically, is why some thought is called for when one is creating an imaginary world. If you feel a certain timidity about the whole undertaking, and that is perfectly natural, you can proceed one little step at a time. Suppose, for example, you have a world with a fairly primitive society whose fastest means of transport is the esroh (horse spelt backwards). Further, suppose that the inhabitants of your world are nomads and have to travel right around it every year to keep pace with the seasons. All right, you give the matter some thought and decide that a horse (sory, esroh) can't be expected to do more than fifty miles a day.

Almost at once you have an idea of the size of your DIY world. If you give it a year of, say, 300 days, it follows that its circumference is 300 multiplied by 50, which equals 15,000 miles. Divide by *pi* to get the diameter and you arrive at a figure of roughly 4,800 miles – not much larger than

Mars. Already, starting off from only two fictional premises, you know quite a bit about your home-made planet. Detail upon detail can be procured in this way – not only in astronomical background, but in geology, biology, botany, and so on.

Starting from what we have said, it would be possible to decide on the type and size of the sun, the mean distance of your planet from the sun, the range of temperatures, the variety of seasons, and so on. If you can cope with the mathematics (and I confess that I can't) then go ahead and make the most of your skill. If you can't do the sums, then get hold of one of those experts whom you have been plying with lemonade, and unleash him and his beloved computer on the problem. But never go over the top, never burden yourself and the reader with expository lumps.

An alternative is make educated guesses, to do what seems right to you and has a commonsense, natural feel to it, and to avoid the 'conspicuous show of scientific accuracy'. The main thing is to make use of your artistic judgement. Go for what your informed instinct tells you is your own personal best. As I said before, any writer who is not striving for perfection is wasting his life.

Worlds upon worlds

I have no fear of heights. In my days as a structural engineer I was quite happy to walk along narrow steel beams at a lethal height above the ground. I was at ease in those circumstances because of being in conscious control of the situation – I knew I wasn't going to be clumsy enough to fall off. But at night, when drifting off to sleep, I would sometimes break out in a sweat when imagining the consequences of one slip on a patch of oil or ice. It eventually came to me that, although I had no fear of heights, I had a great dread of *falling*.

What has that to do with inventing imaginary worlds?

Well, I'm leading up to examples of how a simple gut feeling, common to every member of the human race, can result in a successful work of science fiction, one which leads to the creation of a brand-new environment.

A good way of producing a story of compelling interest is to place a character in a situation which the reader would *hate* to share. Falling from a great height, knowing the inevitable outcome, screaming as the last seconds of your life flash by, must be one of the worst ways to go. Having latched on to that, I became enamoured of writing a novel in which the characters had an ever-present risk of taking the big drop, and in which every now and then, by the law of averages, one of them was bound to make that awful plunge. (The notion was quite legitimate in science-fiction terms because it featured specific otherness. We all live what are essentially two-dimensional lives on the surface of the planet, and so by adding *verticality* I was fulfilling the obligations of a speculative writer.)

My first shot was a novel called *Vertigo* – later expanded and reissued as *Terminal Velocity* – which dealt with our society in a near future where sf's long-cherished dream of personal flight had come true. It looked at the difficulties which would crop up when all citizens (criminals and juvenile delinquents included) could strap on anti-gravity belts and fly through the night at hundreds of miles an hour. Traffic control is a serious problem today, but . . . Just think of it!

The book was fine with me as far as it went, but its inhabitants could fall only for a mile or two. That might give them a couple of minutes to reflect on their unfortunate fates, but I, consumed by the sf writer's professional greed, craved an environment in which the poor souls could fall for hours, or even *days*, with nothing to do but anticipate the final impact.

Not a very honourable motivation, I admit, but the point is that it was the first tiny step in the creation of a new imaginary planetary system.

I kept the idea on the back boiler for a long time, and was beginning to wonder if it could ever be given any kind of veracity. Then one day, while idly glancing through an atlas of the solar system, I happened to notice the peculiar relationship between our outermost planet, Pluto, and its single moon, Charon. The two are quite similar in size, and Charon revolves around Pluto at a surface-to-surface distance of only 15,000 kilometres – less than the distance from Britain to Australia. Furthermore, Charon hangs above the same spot on Pluto – an awe-inspiring sight for the notional inhabitants of either body.

That was all that was needed!

I had seen those facts on paper a few times before, but not until that occasion did the Brownies in the subconscious go into action. In that single moment I saw the universe of what was to become *The Ragged Astronauts* trilogy in its entirety, though without details as yet. The sister worlds of Land and Overland were there, only a few thousand miles apart, each hanging at a fixed point in the other's sky, occupying a large portion of the heavens, with seas and continents clearly visible, looming, beckoning . . .

And that was where the real planning of the book began.

Built into the original inspiration was the idea of a journey from Land to Overland, and I wanted it to be an *epic* journey. In other words, it had to be done by people whose science was barely up to it. That premise fixed the inhabitants of Land at a level of technology roughly equal to seventeenth-century Europe. And it brought the first major problem.

Even if assisted by low gravity, the voyagers would be

unequal to the task of crossing an interplanetary vacuum, so I chose to envelope both worlds in a common atmosphere. Once that was done, I could then visualise the journey being accomplished in hot-air balloons . . .

Do you see what I mean about proceeding one step at a time? Starting from nothing more than an uneasy thought about falling off a steel girder, I ended up with an unusual story which took a third of a million words in the telling. Each decision as it was made then created the framework in which a further decision had to be made, and I eventually reached a detailed picture of a planet, its geography, its flora and fauna, its people and their history. And because it was done gradually, step by reasonable step, it did not take an extraordinary talent or a superhuman effort.

Cryptic clues

A bonus for the sf writer is that the reader tends to have had a lot of previous experience on alien worlds, thus allowing the writer, if it suits his artistic aim, to be very economical with words. In short stories the writer can actually be quite cryptic, relying on his audience to pick up tiny clues and interpret them correctly.

In one of my very short stories I instantaneously transported a character to a distant planet. All that was required to establish the new locale as alien was the following part-sentence: 'Here and there were potted palms which swayed continuously despite the absence of any breeze . . .'

That's all that was really necessary – the educated reader immediately seized on to the fact that the trees were not ordinary potted palms. They could sway by themselves, and therefore the scene was not taking place on Earth. This kind of shorthand is not only appreciated by the reader – it provides intriguing mental exercise for the writer, and is much more fun than doing crossword puzzles.

Lost in space

Not all distant-space stories are set on orthodox planets – i.e. large balls of solid matter in orbit around the sun. The sf writer can exercise his ingenuity by having his characters, human or otherwise, exist in environments which are radically different from what *we* treat as the norm.

Larry Niven's *Ringworld* and my own *Orbitsville* series, as their names might suggest, are respectively set on a vast ring and on a shell which surrounds a sun, the inhabitants living on the inner surfaces. Other stories have used the incredibly bizarre and hostile surface of a neutron star as a setting, and I can remember one whose characters actually lived on the surface of our own sun. (In good sf style, they refused to believe that intelligent life could exist on anything as cold as a planet.) Going to the limits, James Blish, in his 1952 story 'Surface Tension', had a group of space travellers crash on a world which was so hostile to life that they survived only by having the super-computerised ship redesign them as tiny marine life forms. Their descendants, inspired by vague legends about what had happened, wanted to continue the exploration of space, and the story describes their first journey to a neighbouring 'world'. Only at the end do we discover that all they have done is travel from one puddle to another in a ship the size of a peanut.

The last mentioned is an example of the mysterious-environment story, which is a popular sub-variety in sf. In this kind of yarn the author chooses a really outlandish setting, or set of circumstances, one which is often complicated and ingenious. The essence of the technique is that the environment and circumstances are not explained at the beginning. In other words, the author knows what's going on, every character in the story knows what's going on – only the reader is kept in the dark. As the plot gradually unfolds, the author coyly unveils one corner of the mystery after another until, near the end, *all is revealed*.

As I said, many readers enjoy stories cast in this mould. They like being tantalised and being challenged to outguess the writer, so there is no commercial reason for the beginning writer to avoid that literary method if it appeals to him. My unease comes when that sort of thing is taken to the extreme, when the author is obviously seen in the role of a conjurer, whipping a series of pre-planted cards out of his sleeve.

I exclude from this category stories in which the setting is a genuine, alien, baffling, complicated mystery – such as Christopher Priest's *Inverted World* – which both deserves and requires a lengthy investigation. My objection is to those mysterious environments which are mysterious only because of a certain amount of finagling on the author's part.

The standard writing technique in this century is for the hero, the viewpoint character, to be literally that – a kind of roving camera. The reader sees only what the hero sees, hears only what the hero hears, knows only what the hero knows, and so forth. It is a good technique. Everything would fall apart if there was a requirement for the reader to know, via the hero, everything that the *author* knows. But, nevertheless, my instinct says there should be a feeling that the author *also* is on a voyage into the unknown and unexpected. It is best when the reader regards himself as being on a level footing with all others as far as information is concerned. That way, when the events of the story come rolling over him, he has the same feeling as in real life – that they were truly unpredictable, that they were inevitable, that there was nothing he could have done to dodge out of the way.

What on earth are you up to?

Our own familiar, humdrum birthplace can also become an 'alien' world by several means. The most obvious is travel into the future, where the environment has changed because of progress or degeneration. The past, which one might regard as the domain of the historical novelist, is also wide open to the sf writer. Then there is the 'alternate world' or 'alternate universe' story, in which a multiplicity of Earths exist side by side in time, each differing in one respect from its neighbour.

The last mentioned is also known as the 'parallel time stream' story, although a pedant might say 'divergent time stream'. I'm sorry about all these labels, but the very fact of their existence shows that science fiction gives one a lot to think about. There is, also, a connection between the latter two categories. If one is inclined to accept the basic concept of time travel, there is little to quibble about in the notion of jumping forwards. The future has not happened yet, therefore it is malleable and can be altered at will.

The past, obviously, is a different matter, and brings in the famous time-travel paradox. If Fred went back in time and killed his grandfather, then Fred's father would never have been born, and Fred himself could never have been born – so how could he have gone back and killed his grandfather? (It reveals quite a lot about our culture that the paradox is never presented in terms of Fred going back and killing either his own direct parents or his grand*mother*.) The escape route is to consider time as being something like a stream, and at the point where the homicidal Fred suddenly pops up, the stream is forced to split in two. In one branch the future continues on its normal course; in the other Fred *does* kill his grandfather, but the 'proper' future is unaffected.

The idea of time being a river, or rather a vast delta, has some philosophical credence, and the science-fiction mind is naturally drawn to it. Who can resist the notion of time splitting at every decision point there ever was, thus creating an infinite number of universes? The woman who, for most of her days has regretted marrying Dull Dave when she could have had Sparky Simon instead, can console herself with the thought that in another universe she *did* marry Simon and is having a life of constant excitement with him. She might not consider the possibility that, simultaneously, her other self has become a nervous wreck because of Simon's impetuosity, and is cursing herself for not having had enough commonsense to marry Dave. But that's science fiction for you.

By extending the above thinking we reach the 'alternate history' story, where time has divided at some crucial point quite far into the past. The story is always set in the 'other' time stream, i.e. not in our 'proper' stream, and the attraction is largely in the convincing extrapolation of a different version of reality. This is a major division of science fiction, one which gives writers a great opportunity to exercise their imaginations and display erudition. Basically, it is the game of 'What If?' in its ultimate form.

What would the world be like today if the Nazis had won World War II? That example, because it is lurking in everybody's subconscious, is so obvious that not much use is made of it in sf – but the possibilities abound. What if Columbus had lost his nerve and turned back? What if the Roman Empire had not collapsed? What if the dinosaur family had not become extinct? What if Leonardo da Vinci had succeeded in inventing a practicable flying machine?

The writer is free to go to any turning point in history, major or minor, and from there steer his own course through time's delta. Devotees of this class of story particularly enjoy themselves when the chosen divergent point is one which at first appears to be insignificant, and in which the author has used high ingenuity in devising and developing the knock-on consequences. I have already mentioned the time traveller who dropped a cigarette end in London in 1666, but the story most quoted is Ray Bradbury's 'A Sound of Thunder', in which the chrononaut, visiting the Paleocene era, accidentally kills a butterfly and thus changes the entire course of our history.

That example is frivolous, of course, but alternate history stories are often vehicles for serious comment on defects in society. By portraying the way things might have been they give us new insights into the way things *are*.

There is excellent opportunity here for the new writer who is well versed in some aspect of history, or is prepared to do the necessary reading, but – as always – it is important to keep the background of your story *in* the background. Victorian London has featured in quite a few recent novels, some written by Americans, who, eager to build up a sense of place, and perhaps to make use of research data, tended to lay the local colour on too thickly. Almost every paragraph contained street names, beggars and toffs, coach wheels clattering on cobblestones, and fog rolling up from the greasy Thames. By contrast, it is interesting to look at books set in and around Victorian London, by writers of the period – such as Doyle, Jerome and the Grossmith brothers – who knew the setting well. Their work is known for its evocation of the time and place, and yet very *little* wordage is expended on background, the occasional illuminating detail doing the trick.

The main reason for the economy may have been that they were utterly familiar with the setting, and expected their readership to be likewise. The sf writer and his audience are in the opposite situation, *but that is all the more reason for using a similar sparse style.* Verisimilitude can be achieved by goading the reader's imagination with just a few words, contriving for it to do the hard work on your behalf. Hints can be more effective than plain statements; what you leave out can be more important than what you keep in.

If, in the description of a future society, there is an offhand reference to a woman wearing an expensive perfume called Roast Beef, or Fried Ham, it can be deduced that we are in a world which has become desperately short of proteins. Not only that, but while the reader is assimilating the fact that an entire perfume industry has sprung up around people's craving for meat, he will be prompted to envisage a great amount of complementary infrastructure – perhaps even to try beating the author at his own game. He won't *be* beating the author, of course – he will simply be joining the author's team, and that's what you want.

Abacus for sale, batteries not included

A technique we touched on earlier – turning the reader's expectations upside down – is particularly useful and rewarding in time-travel stories. It can be employed with serious or humorous intent, but on the whole seems to lend itself more readily to the latter.

It is only to be expected that a man from today who finds himself hurled into the past will have a technological advantage over his new contemporaries. But will he? Similarly, a man displaced forwards in time should not be able to function effectively in the sophisticated society of the future. But will that be the case?

A classic in this respect is L. Sprague de Camp's 1939

novel, *Lest Darkness Fall*, in which an involuntary time traveller finds himself in sixth-century Rome and does his best to forestall the coming of the Dark Ages. Much of the humour in the book stems from the hero failing where he expects to succeed, or succeeding where he expects to fail, when confronted with the technology of the times.

A favourite of mine is Dean McLaughlin's 1968 novella, *Hawk Among the Sparrows*, in which the pilot of an ultra-modern jet fighter cruising over present-day Europe is thrown back in time to the closing months of World War I. He *knows* that his single plane has enough fire power to wipe out what is left of the German air force, but there is nothing but frustration in store for him. His smart missiles can't seek out the enemy aircraft because the latter's engines don't emit enough heat; and he can't make regular sorties because his engines run on kerosene, which at the time is used only as a cooking fuel. The final straw comes when he is forced to try flying a current-model biplane and is completely unable to handle it.

Putting it the other way round, you can have a person displaced into the future and doing exceptionally well for himself, perhaps because of a robust constitution, or because his blunt, untutored ways cut through the unnecessary sophistication which surrounds him.

Science fiction is already rich in the kinds of story discussed above, but the scope is so vast that the beginning writer should not be discouraged from making his own special contribution.

7

THE THREE Rs – ROCKETSHIPS,
RAYGUNS AND ROBOTS

The dear old rocketship, in the pattern favoured by Flash
Gordon, used to be an indispensable part of science fiction.
There was a time when practically all one needed to set up
in business as an sf writer was a facility for describing rocket
exhausts – a flair for flares, if you like. In these Model Ts
of the astronautics world, 'sky jockeys' used to blast, blaze,
torch, burn or otherwise incinerate their way up from the
Earth's surface to our neighbouring planets, and even to
the stars.

It is possible to become quite nostalgic about those old
stories, even though they provide yet another example of
how science fiction failed to get its predictions anywhere
near the mark. All right, we forecast interplanetary travel,
but people have been doing that for centuries as a kind of
knee-jerk of the imagination, ever since the notion of other
worlds entered the general consciousness. It would have
been gratifying if science-fiction writers had managed to get
even one detail right before real-life space technologists
rubbed their noses in it.

The 1950 film *Destination Moon*, scripted by Robert
Heinlein, was regarded as a very good approximation of how
things would actually be – but in retrospect it is laughable. In
the following year George Pal made *When Worlds Collide*,

in which a handful of people escape by spaceship from a doomed Earth. The only successful working example of a rocket that had been seen until then was the German V2, and sf artists of the day were enamoured of its mathematically pure lines, so Pal's escape ship was a silvery, tarted-up V2. The fact that the V2 was designed to crash nose first into the ground at supersonic speed – hardly compatible with the idea of escaping from peril – was not really given much consideration.

The purpose of all the above is not to denigrate the sf practitioners of old, but to give reassurance to newcomers who may fear that the subject of space flight, so central to sf, will be too much for them.

You can't get there from here

As mentioned in a previous chapter, science-fiction writers are finding life progressively more difficult on all the worlds and moons of the solar system. Many stories have yet to be written with those settings, but the going is getting tough for authors whose inclination is not towards really hard sf. At the heart of the problem is the fact that rockets – vessels which progress by shooting matter out of their rear ends at high speed – are not much use for getting around the galaxy.

The built-in snag with conventional rockets is that they have to carry their own propellants. The weight of the fuel is a major limiting factor in today's long-range jets, but with a rocket intended to reach distant stars we would be talking in millions of tons, which is obviously not a sensible proposition. A step further on from ordinary rockets we reach the interstellar ram-jet. These vessels use huge electromagnetic fields to scoop up the micro-dust that floats through all of space. This material is then used as reaction mass, discharged out the back at very high velocity, thus avoiding the need to carry all those mega-tons of fuel. An interstellar ram-jet would probably be of convenient dimensions – possibly about the size of a present-day car ferry – but it would never able to reach C (the speed of light) and the journey to a star would still be measured in decades, even under the most favourable circumstances.

One way around this difficulty is to accept the limitations and meet them head-on. This leads you to what is known as the 'generation ship' story, in which the ship puts on a quick burst of speed at the start of the journey and then coasts to its target world, just as today's space probes do. It will take many centuries to reach a star by this method, so those on board must resign themselves to the fact that only their descendants, many generations later, will see the destination. To me this has always seemed a rather sombre idea, and I have never written about generation ships, but there is nothing to stop new authors injecting freshness into it. A word of warning here: do not attempt a story in which the travellers gradually forget about their origins and start believing that the ship is their home planet. I'm not saying it is impossible to revive that plot, but to do so would take a *lot* of expertise and talent.

Another way of dealing with slow ships is to put the crew into suspended animation for the duration of the voyage. That idea has a certain amount of sense to it, and can still be made good use of, though generally speaking the voyage has to be completed without incident, and the events of the story confined to planetary settings at either end. Not a great deal can be done with a row of frozen bodies, and the limited avenues of action have been pretty well explored.

Stand aside, Mr Einstein – you're blocking the way

What I'm getting around to saying, is that when NASA gradually drove sf writers off our neighbouring worlds, we put up with it, because you can't argue with cameras and scientific measuring instruments. With some grumbling, it must be said, we agreed to pack up and move to planets orbiting other stars – and then Albert Einstein chipped in, with his famous equation, and told us we couldn't even do that!

If we had meekly accepted the dictate that nothing can go faster than light, much good science fiction would have been reduced to the status of fairy stories, or would never have been written at all. It is essential to the genre that we have the ability to transport people among the stars with journey times that can conveniently be measured in days, or hours, or seconds. In extreme cases, the trip should take no time at all.

That is why, over the years, sf writers have exercised much ingenuity in finding ways around the Einstein Barrier. It is all part of the Secret Game. Everybody involved *knows* that FTL (faster than light) travel is impossible, but as long as the writer puts in a few lines to acknowledge that the problem exists the reader will be satisfied and will play along. Most of the wordage will be gobbledegook, but it is nice when one can produce *good* gobbledegook. The following are some of the methods which have given excellent service, have become standard sf currency and are available to the beginning writer.

First and foremost is the warp drive, which at first was mainly used as a method of instantaneous travel. The idea was this: imagine that a tiny snail is on one corner of a big piece of paper and is determined to reach the opposite corner. In normal circumstances the journey would take quite a long time, but you could help the snail by folding

114

the paper over, corner to corner, and waiting until the little fellow has crossed from one to the other. When you straighten the paper out again the snail will find himself at his destination without having crossed the intervening space. To you it was a simple piece of manipulation, but to the snail it will have seemed like a miracle and he will probably puzzle over it for the rest of his life.

Warp drives operate in the same way. The pilot energises some kind of 'geometry distorter matrix' – thus bending space like our piece of paper – makes a few adjustments, switched off again and, *voila*! the ship is at its destination.

That kind of drive is really good for getting around the universe, but it has a drawback in that nothing can happen during the voyage. It is over as soon as it has started. One of the best known pseudo-laws of sf is that pilots can never go into warp drive in the vicinity of a planet. The official explanation is either that the drive wouldn't work properly, or that it would do terrible damage to the planet. But the *real* reason is that it forces ships to proceed conventionally for a while, during which they can be chased, shot at, struck by meteors, sabotaged, intercepted, etc.

Science fiction depends so much on control bridge scenes, meetings with other ships, and so on, that the original warp drive was very soon modified to one with which the journeys took an appreciable and convenient length of time. When Captain Kirk's *Enterprise* goes into 'warp factor eight' we know that *something* is being warped, even if there is some dispute about what it actually is, and the ship is enabled to fly at many times the speed of light.

One explanation is that such a ship 'rotates' itself into another 'dimension' or 'frame of reference' where the speed of light is very much greater than it is in our continuum. There the ship can exceed C without contravening Einstein's laws. The names for this region are various – subspace, the fourth or fifth dimension, hyperspace, null space, are all popular – and the reader is accustomed to them. A line such as 'the star cruiser emerged in normal space' speaks volumes.

Chief pioneer of the interstellar epic was Dr E. E. Smith, who was at his creative peak in the second quarter of this century. Although he qualified as a food chemist, and specialised in doughnut mixtures, 'Doc' Smith's scientific turn of mind led to the beautiful invention of the 'inertialess drive'. The inertia of a body is what makes it difficult for you to move it from rest, or to stop it once it gets properly going, and Smith got great mileage from this concept.

Depriving a body of its inertia would entail depriving it of its mass, in which case it would cease to exist altogether, but Smith did not worry about trivia – instead he concentrated on giving his audience maximum enjoyment. A spaceship with no mass could travel at thousands of times the speed of light, unimpeded by Einstein, but it was the absence of inertia which gave Smith the greatest chance to stir our sense of wonder.

If the commanders of two spaceships, going in opposite directions at a million miles a second, wanted to rendezvous with each other, all they had to do was to crash head on. With no inertia to contend with, the ships simply came to a halt on the spot without even a pencil or a coffee mug sliding off a table. In spite of an interval of forty long years, I vividly remember that priceless, cool tingling along the spine which the sf buff experiences when an intellectual crowbar forces his mind to expand.

Full speed ahead

As I hope you are beginning to see, the business of getting your characters from star to star in a short time is wide open. Anybody can have a go. American writer Lester del Rey used to boast that he thought up a different rationale for faster-than-light travel in every space story he wrote – and there was a lot of them.

To give a further example, imagine that you have a time machine large enough to accommodate a spaceship. The stars are in constant motion, the galaxy rotates, the myriad galaxies of the observable universe are flying apart. So, if you activate your machine and step outside normal time for a hundred or a thousand years, when you re-enter time you might be a long way in space from where you started.

That would undoubtedly be a risky way of getting from A to B, but to my mind not half as dangerous as the modern fad for diving one's ship into a black hole. Theorists have come up with the notion that black holes could be entrances to 'wormholes' in space, and that a ship dropping into one of them could pop up in another part of the universe. Somehow, I have my doubts. It lingers in my mind that black holes were given that label only because they *appear* like holes in space. In fact, they are the *opposite* of holes – balls of matter so condensed that a piece the size of a tennis ball could weigh as much as the Earth. I have this sneaking suspicion that anybody naive enough to dive into a black hole would simply go *splat*!, but when reading sf or watching a movie I go along with the rules of the Secret Game.

As a final instance of what can be done with FTL, let's use the true and tried sf technique of standing a concept on its head. The difficulty with interstellar travel is that the distances are so great – but what if the distances were very *small*? Only a few inches? The way to achieve that is to make the ship and its crew very large. Instead of switching on a warp drive they activate the 'exponential dimension modifier', and instantly the ship and its crew are as big as the galaxy. They can see millions of stars floating all around them *inside the ship* like dust motes in sunlight. In the

117

control room there is a set of cross-hairs. The commander, using the ship's micro-jets, delicately moves his vessel only a few inches, until the cross-hairs intersect close to the target star. He then switches off the EDM and the ship snaps back to its normal size. All is as before – except that the ship is now hundreds of light years from its starting point, and the sun that blazes in the view screens is an alien star . . .

In one book, *Ship of Strangers*, I carried that system to extremes and had a ship which inadvertently became bigger than the entire universe. If you're going to feature an accident you might as well pick a good one. The ship began shrinking slowly, which gave rise to scenes like the following:

A continuous rain of galaxies was spraying up through the floor, passing through the table and chairs and human beings, and out through the ceiling into the vessel's upper levels. The galaxies looked like slightly fuzzy stars to the naked eye, but when examined with a magnifying glass they were seen to be perfect little lens-shapes or spirals, miniature jewels being squandered into space by an insane creator.

Surgenor sat at the long table, bemused, watching the motes of light passing through his own arms and hands, and tried to comprehend that each one contained a hundred billion suns or more . . .

The point of all the above is that if you really need to go to the stars, all you have to do is *go*. The reader will be happy to go with you.

Futuristic weaponry

The heading of this section is probably something of a misnomer as far as sf on the screen is concerned. Anybody who watches the violet pantomimes which Hollywood passes off as science fiction must have noticed that the guns have become *bigger* and *heavier* – something which is contrary to the general run of technology. It appears that bulky machine guns, which at the beginning of this century were sensibly mounted on tripods, will in the future be supported by bulging muscles alone. The same biceps-and-blasters trend is evident in the comics, which are starting to be known – slightly defensively – as graphic novels.

When designing spaceships the author is always striving for improvements, but that is not the case with military equipment. The sf writer has a vested interest in keeping his imagined weaponry at a comparatively primitive level. If the handgun had been allowed to progress at the speed allowed for other science-fictional hardware, the familiar six-shooter would soon have become a lightweight, pocket-sized object. It would probably be silent in operation, and totally effective. When someone points it at a soldier and presses the button that soldier will die for sure; when the focus is widened and the button pressed again a whole platoon or even a regiment will die for sure. Instantly, quietly and neatly.

I hope that by now you have gleaned enough about plotting in sf to foresee the problems posed by these perfect weapons. If they were brought into everyday science-fictional use – as are computers, robots, matter transmitters, etc. – quite a lot of stories would never get written. Filmed sf, in particular, would suffer – most of today's offerings depend on the use of weapons which look impressive and make a lot of noise but hardly ever achieve the desired result. Even Benny and Mal, last seen on that airless

119

asteroid, would have been seriously affected, one or the other expiring in the first few pages.

The above considerations make life difficult for the sf writer, but the situation is not hopeless, especially if you are prepared to take up the challenge to your imagination and go all out to find something new. It is important to remember that, generally speaking, the primary purpose of a weapon is not to kill another person – but to force him to go along with your plans. I hate people who commit robbery with violence, but am prepared to grant them the benefit of the doubt and assume that, given a free choice, they would give up firearms for neat, silent instruments which would cause people to fall into a harmless unconsciousness for thirty minutes.

Even if a criminal was worried about witnesses, a gun which erased the day's memory would be all that was necessary – and the penalty would be less than that for murder. Science fiction offers possibilities in this general line of imaginative weaponry which are well worth exploring. American writer A.E. van Vogt, who was a leading figure in the genre in the 1940s and 50s, came up with the idea of guns which would fire only in self-defence. Eric Frank Russell, for one of his early books, invented a truly nasty and effective handgun. It was silent, and occasioned the victim no immediate pain or obvious injury, but it caused some of his blood to clot. He would die of coronary thrombosis, but that would be some time later – by which time the assassin was long departed from the scene.

The point is that there is no need to give up the sheer nastiness and fiendishness and blood-thirstiness which adds spice to many narratives, especially those in which you want a really evil character to tax the hero's wits and make him look good. What I'm saying is that for the honour of our craft you should put the imagination to work and equip your characters with more interesting hardware than was available to Buffalo Bill or Al Capone. And, as a bonus, there is the chance of getting a better story out of it.

Metal manservants?

In science fiction the word 'robot' tends to refer to an intelligent machine which can get around by itself, preferably on two legs. A robot which progressed by employing wheels or caterpillar treads would somehow be unsatisfactory. It is the robot's attempt to walk like a man which betrays its ambition to *be* a man, or at least supplant him. The emotions aroused by that ungodly yearning were what made the robot a mainstay of printed science fiction for many years. We either felt smugly secure and a little sympathetic – 'Fancy a poor assemblage of gears and transistors aspiring to our near-divine status!'; or we began to feel threatened and said, 'My God, what if that soulless mannikin – incapable of feeling pain or pity – actually got the upper hand?'

Science-fiction writers seized on the double-edged theme and produced thousands of stories, some of them among the best that have appeared in the genre. Asimov's laws of robotics are known to people who would not regard themselves as sf readers. Clifford D. Simak's wonderful 'City' series succeeded in bringing tears to my young eyes with its poignant depiction of men, dogs and robots forming a partnership to face a future which was increasingly inimical to the most cherished human values.

The snag as far as the beginning sf writer is concerned is that the familiar old robot has just about been done to death. Much of the difficulty springs from the growing realisation that designing and manufacturing an effective man-like robot is just about impossible. Automation and the science of artificial intelligence have come a long way since

Karel Capek introduced the robot idea, in a play first produced in Prague in 1921, but even now we are incapable of
making a machine – no matter how large – which could go
out on its own and perform a simple task like sweeping a
town's gutters.

It should be noted that man-like robots are divided into
two classes: humanoids, which, in spite of having the general
configuration of humans, are still obviously machines; and
androids, which cannot readily be distinguished from
humans. If the android robot is ever to become a reality it
will be in the *far*-distant future, but a question remains:
what on earth would be the point in its existence? After all,
when we want our clothes washed we entrust them to a
primitive robot – one which is white, rectangular and has a
round window in front. We don't expect a mechanical servant, perhaps wearing a frilly apron, to gather our undies
into its arms and then wash them in a tub.

The whole notion of androids is a leftover from the early
nineteenth century when the technology of the day first
made it possible to manufacture clockwork dummies as
showpieces which could excite the wonder of a crowd by
raising their arms or turning their heads. To the naive mind
(I have to be a little condescending here, although I'm sure
I would have gladly been suckered at the time), the next
step was a fully functional artificial human being.

To any thinking writer of today that idea is, not to put
too fine a point on it, daft. The only place where it is still
given any kind of credence is Hollywood, which for the
most part is creeping towards the stage occupied by printed
sf in about 1940. The homicidal, near-indestructible android
robot is ideal for the futuristic pantomime of violence, but
I would advise the new science-fiction writer to try employing his imagination and talent to better effect.

A basic counter to fearsome robots was the cute, lovable,
accident-prone and otherwise quirky type. That reaction

was what provided *Star Wars* with R2D2 and C3PO – the Abbott and Costello of robotics. Again, film was far behind print, the comic aspect of robots having been targeted since 1950 by writers such as Henry Kuttner, Robert Sheckley, Brian Aldiss and Harry Harrison. The vein has been mined pretty thoroughly by now, but there is gold in it yet for the inventive writer with a talent for humour.

The ubiquitous computer

When one tries in the imagination to jump ahead of actual technological development, it often turns out that it is the most difficult-seeming part of a problem which those pesky scientists and engineers – who obviously don't read enough sf – succeed in solving first. Forty years ago, when such computers as existed were about the size of a small bungalow, I would have predicted that the tricky bit in building a roughly man-like robot would have been the brain. Having seen what has happened in the meantime, I am becoming reconciled to the idea of a robotic computer-brain some day fitting into a small container. (Robots have the advantage over humans in this respect – it might be more logical, and safer, for the brain to be tucked away in the chest cavity.)

Recent achievements in computer development have been truly stupendous, and are continuing at an accelerating pace. Many sf writers and readers are fascinated by computers, and today – especially in shorter work – it is possible to sell stories which seem to consist of little *but* computer terminology. If your inclinations are in that direction this is the time to dive in and make as big a splash as you can.

It is worth remembering, however, that many people *don't* care about how computers work and find the whole subject quite dull. That being the case, keep in mind the fact that for most technological products the trend is that year by year they become *easier* to use. Early in this century the humble radio set was so complicated and full of mystery that hotels employed experts to stand in the lobby and conjure music from the air for the benefit of guests. It isn't so long ago that making a video recording was an operation that required a gang of BBC engineers and a room full of expensive equipment.

The way things are going in the electronics world, it will fairly soon be possible to have computers the size of postage stamps, which will adhere to the wrist; or like small beads which can be worn in the ear. Operating them will not require a course of study and long sessions at the keyboard. If you need to find out how many Lithuanian nationals are working in Iceland, you will simply say, 'Computer, how many Lithuanian nationals are working in Iceland?' The computer will reply, 'Seven', and that will be the end of it.

That prospect, it seems to me, is one to be welcomed by the science-fiction writer. I have often been impressed by an author's display of computer know-how, but there is a limit to how long one can stand in awe of such things. I quite like the thought of computers being shoved into the background a bit more, thus clearing the stage for the really interesting characters in any drama – the human beings.

8

BRINGING ALL THE THREADS TOGETHER

A difficulty I had in writing this book was that the subjects insisted on trying to spread out from underneath the headings I had so carefully assigned to them. I am regarding that as a good sign. In fact, I have decided to regard it as a *very* good sign – writing has infinite variety, it is an art as much as a craft, and it doesn't meekly submit to being crammed into compartments. Science fiction, in particular, tends to be a bit unruly in this respect. If the idea for a story can be elevated to the status of a character, and if the background can be more important than the foreground – what does that do to one's categories?

In this chapter, therefore, and before we discuss taking your story to market, I will deal with a number of subjects which, although vital in themselves, can't really be allocated separate chapters. The first one deserves to be first, because it concerns the reader's initial contact point with your story – the title.

What's in a name?

The answer to that question, especially in the case of a short story, is a hell of a lot. It has been said that it is possible to sell a short story on the basis of a good title, a good opening paragraph and a good ending paragraph. That may be something of an exaggeration, but there is little doubt that a good title will play an important part in the success of a shorter piece of fiction.

It is a matter of word-length, the perceived bulk of the work. A prospective reader may notice a thick volume on the bookseller's shelves and see that it is called *Oliver Twist*. That isn't much of a title, he may think, but so much wordage has gone into the idea behind it that there must be *something* there worth looking at.

Things are different where the short story is concerned, especially in a literary climate in which the strongly plotted story is often looked upon with disfavour by the establishment. The reader is wary of being short-changed, because it has happened to him so often in the past, and he relies on the title for guidance. When he picks up a magazine or an anthology – unless first drawn by the name of an author – he will turn to the story which has the best title.

By 'best' I mean any good selection from, or permutation of, adjectives such as 'striking', 'intriguing', 'mysterious'. 'humorous', 'inventive', 'erotic', 'cynical', 'poetic', 'emotional', 'clever', 'sinister', 'scholarly' . . . The list could go on, although not much further. I would be very happy if I could at this point trot out a rule of thumb or well-tried formula for creating good titles, but life isn't as easy as that for an author.

Thinking up a really good title is usually very hard work, and can be frustrating in the extreme. There have been times when I have had a completed work – novel or shorter piece – sitting around for days, all ready to go into the post and bring me some money, and everything has ground to a halt because of my inability to come up with the right title. Sometimes, in the end, out of sheer desperation I have stuck down some fairly arbitrary combination of words, and have had to live with the result ever since . . .

It can happen that a really nice title will spring to mind along with the original inspiration for a story, but when it doesn't – which is most of the time – you should look out for your chance during the actual writing. Keep the heart of your story in mind, the *essence*, and seek a word or combination of words which directly relate to it without giving the game away. Often it can be enough to find a single word which evokes the mood of a story, but titles such as 'Twilight' and 'Futility' are running into short supply.

The great stand-by for title seekers is the literary or poetic quotation, and the resources are so extensive that it is unlikely that they will ever be mined out. It can be very frustrating, however, after you have settled down with your reference books, to discover just how *much* of Shakespeare has been already been parcelled up into three- or four-word lots and flogged off as ready-made titles. A search through the major poets usually yields a good result, though, and there is no way of estimating the number of sf writers who have cursed Bradbury for getting to ' – And the Moon Be Still as Bright' before they did. It is almost as if the words had been penned with a moody, romantic sf story in mind, and it is surprising how often the great writers have been similarly obliging.

Another good device, although it requires excellent judgement, is to invent a title which actually does encapsulate the idea of the story – but the reader doesn't appreciate that fact until afterwards. Ideally, he should finish the story with a contented sigh, and then be struck by the appositeness of the title. 'That guy (fill in your own name here) is a crafty so-and-so,' the reader should think. 'I'm going to look out for more of his work.'

One example from the many is Dannie Plachta's 'Revival Meeting', in which a terminally ill man pays his fortune to have his body cryogenically preserved. The familiar plan is that he can be woken up again in the distant future, when medical science has advanced to the stage at which his illness can be cured. When he is eventually brought round again he is told to rest in preparation for the heart transplant. He asks what is wrong with his heart. 'Nothing,' says the figure looming over him, 'but there's something wrong with mine.'

That scene was implicit in the title, but the sardonic humour doesn't become apparent until afterwards.

Ray Bradbury (yes, his name does keep cropping up) did a similar thing in a short story about the way in which the murder rate in places like New York increases dramatically during the summer, when the terrible heat and humidity drive people mad. The story was called 'It's Not the Heat, It's the Hu . . .' Only after finishing it does one envisage the last word of the title being cut short by a revolver or a knife. That is probably the only example of a title which not only sums up the whole idea contained in a story, but turns it into a seven-word stage play.

Science fiction, because of its range of ideas, offers the author great scope for intriguing titles. Here are three taken more or less at random from the treasure house: 'Can You Feel Anything When I Do This?' (Robert Sheckley); 'The Women Men Don't See ' (James Tiptree Jr); 'Let's Go to Golgotha!' (Garry Kilworth). I submit that anyone who can read the likes of that and not feel a nagging desire to go on and discover what comes next has not got the makings of a science-fiction fan. The writer should feel a complementary challenge to capture the reader's mind.

Everything can be overdone, of course. Science fiction also offers great opportunities for the writer to go over the top in this respect. The title of Samuel R. Delaney's 1967 novelette – 'Time Considered as a Helix of Semi-Precious Stones' – might be forgiven if it had any real connection with the actual narrative. The story won major awards, though, and it is interesting to speculate on how important the title was in attracting readers and thereby pulling in votes.

Playfulness in titles is quite permissible, I'm glad to say, and it often manifests itself in length. Grant Carrington's 1974 four-page story was called 'After You've Stood on a Log at the Center of the Universe, What Is There Left to Do?' Possibly the longest title ever was Michael Bishop's 'On the Street of the Serpents or the Assassination of Chairman Mao as Effected by the Author in Seville, Spain in the Spring of 1992, a Year of No Certain Historicity'. Another abundance came with D.G. Compton's 'Hot Wireless Sets, Aspirin Tablets, the Sandpaper Sides of Used Matchboxes, and Something That Might Have Been Castor Oil'.

Composing titles like those must be a pleasurable pursuit, but there is a need for some restraint. Obviously, a certain amount of editorial compliance was involved in the above concoctions ever seeing the light of day. You don't want to spend hours thinking up a thirty-word title, only to have it honed down to a single word by a tired, unsympathetic or harassed editor. There is no point at all in rocking the boat. The best example of an sf author going out of his way to make life difficult for editors and librarians was when Kurt Vonnegut entitled one of his early short stories 'The Big Space Fuck'. It certainly attracted attention, but the tactic is one I do not recommend.

To repeat my main points, a good title doesn't usually drop into your lap. Do not wait until the story has been written and then decide what to call it. Issue a harsh order to the Brownies down in the subconscious, telling them that you *demand* an excellent title for the work in progress.

Always remember the importance of the title – especially for a short story – and be prepared to *work* for it.

How does this grab you?

It goes without saying that, after the title, the reader's next point of contact with your work is the opening sentence or paragraph. For the reasons advanced above, it is a good idea to give a short story a beginning which grips the reader's attention immediately. This kind of opening is often called a fish-hook or a grabber.

Science fiction, because of its sheer scope, lends itself to the verbal winding and tying of fish-hooks. The idea, of course, is to be mysterious, intriguing and inviting – all in the space of a handful of words. It does no harm consciously to think of yourself as setting a trap for the unwary reader. Your prey may be casually flipping through the pages of a magazine without any intention of actually reading a story – but when he has seen your opening line, taken the bait, he has no option but to go on to the finish.

Some years ago I published a short story called 'A Little Night Flying', which has recently been incorporated in my novel, *Terminal Velocity*. The opening paragraph was:

The dead cop came drifting in towards the Birmingham control zone at a height of some three thousand metres. It was a winter night, and the sub-zero temperature which prevailed at that altitude had solidified his limbs, encrusting the entire body with black frost. Blood flowing through shattered armour had frozen into the semblance of a crab, with its claws encircling his chest. The body, which was in an upright position, rocked gently on stray currents, performing a strange aerial shuffle.

And at its waist a pea-sized crimson light blinked on and off, on and off, its radiance gradually fading under a thickening coat of ice.

I had just written those lines when a friend called at my house for a chat. While I was fetching a drink he wandered over to the typewriter and read the paragraph. He went home soon afterwards. Life continued as usual for a few months, then one day I bumped into my friend in the street. 'All right, Shaw,' was the first thing he said, 'what *was* going on in that damned story?'

Got you! I thought gleefully, enjoying a minor personal triumph. That's the sort of satisfaction you can get from a well-constructed fish-hook, and it is worth spending a good bit of time and effort to produce an effective one. As has already been said, a novel can be more easily trusted to stand on its own without help from the title or opening lines, but sf offers so many opportunities in this respect that novelists quite often respond. And why not? There is no law which states that a 400-page book can't be interesting from the very first line.

'The doorknob opened a blue eye and blinked at him.' That was the opening sentence of Lewis Pagett's *The Fairy Chessmen* a book I read nearly forty years ago, and the fact that I can quote it and its source without consulting a reference work speaks for itself. Christopher Priest began one of his major works, *Inverted World*, with: 'I had reached the age of six hundred and fifty miles.' The most quoted opening sentence in sf is probably the one which George Orwell chose for 1984: 'It was a bright cold day in April and the clocks were striking thirteen.'

I trust that those three examples make the point clear. If you can read them without feeling a yearning to read on and on you are probably in a minority as far as the sf community is concerned. But, again, it is a matter of personal taste and judgement. Some readers might be annoyed by the obvious attempt to capture their interest so quickly; in many cases a writer will deem that a fish-hook is not an appropriate way into the story he has it in mind to write. When the tone of a story is to be one of dignity and seriousness, the fish-hook could indeed be out of place. However, it will still be in the author's interest to commandeer the reader's attention and sympathy right from the start. Pursuing the fish-hook metaphor, you should think about using a *lure*. The writing should be clean and lucid – not cramming too many confusing facts or names into a small space. It should give the impression of leading to something that the reader would be sorry to miss.

The house of science fiction has many mansions.

Footnotes and glossaries

It is important in most sf to create a feeling of authenticity, a topic we touched upon earlier. One time-honoured way of going about this is to use footnotes and glossaries to give your story the look of something which has been densely researched. It worked extremely well with *The Lord of the Rings* – fantasy rather than science fiction, but a good example – and in that case the techique was probably justified because of all the creative years Tolkien had put into the concept and background. It also was appropriate in the old Gernsback-style story, in which the avowed aim was to educate the reader in scientific matters, but the new writer of today is well advised to steer clear of the device.

The exception is when an author has a reputation for deeply researched books, so much so that the paying customer knows the situation in advance and *expects* an educational experience on top of the customary enjoyment of reading a work of fiction. That is another aspect of the Secret Game, and is taking us beyond the natural province of this book.

Another objection to the footnote and glossary trick is that it takes the risk of causing the reader to free himself from the subtle bondage of your words so that he can look something up. It is hard enough to get him mesmerised in the first place without your stepping in wearing your author's hat and saying. 'All right, we will now take a thirty-second break while this reference can be checked.'

The worst form is when the author, in his determination to emphasise the alienness of his invented world, has a character say something like 'Your Highness, I have galloped a full forty *worbles** to meet you.' When you follow the asterisk trail to the bottom of the page you find a note which explains that a *worble* is a unit of length equivalent to half a mile.

The irritating thing is that the entire conversation is being conducted in Dorokian, the language of a planet which is a million light years from Earth, and the only reason we can understand *any* of it is that the author is translating for us. If he has obliged that far, I always cry, why did the silly ass stop short at *worble*? Why didn't he just write 'twenty miles' and have done with it?

Obviously, if a story contains some object or abstraction for which there is absolutely no counterpart here and now, then it *should* be given an invented name. As with the nomenclature for alien characters, the words should look as if they had been thought up by aliens – but not perverse aliens. If you dub an object 'zzythyq' the reader is likely to become irritated when he thinks about pronunciation.

One case in which it is usually necessary to use quite a large number of invented words is when detailing the environs and geography of an inhabited alien world. I always try to dilute what might turn into a torrent of made-up place names by using some which could be universal. 'Yellow River' or 'Greenmount' could crop up anywhere, but of course the world has to have its uniquely local names as well. These should have a 'family trait' look to them, creating a feeling that they have been drawn from a language which you have imagined in its entirety as part of the story's substructure.

One way of achieving this is to make the words corruptions of others with which you are already familiar. You can take a word, stare at it for a while, cut bits off or add bits on, give them a shuffle or two. For that kind of exercise I tend to use titles from a nearby bookcase – thus 'astronomy' gave me the Gulf of Tronom, which was an important location in my *Ragged Astronaut* series of novels.

I have been congratulated on the skill with which I managed to suggest an authentic common source for all the alien names in those books, but have to confess that it was done simply by the technique described above. I was content to use English words as raw material in that case, because the race featured in the novels was culturally close to Britain, but the method can be varied by glancing at foreign books. Other languages use different rules for putting words together, and that will be reflected in the alien names they yield, while at the same time suggesting a coherent family tree. The languages of what was Yugoslavia, for example, are full of words which would fit well in a story practically as they stand.

Linguistics is a complex and difficult science. It has been used as a central element in the construction of many successful stories, but the author needs to be well qualified for the task. The moral for the general sf writer is to use your commonsense in these matters, and don't scatter strange words around merely because of their looks.

Some practical tips on method

One of the weirdest things about the profession of writing is that its practitioners often love it and hate it at the same time. Dorothy McArdle's novel *Uneasy Freehold* was made into a film, *The Uninvited*, which was Hollywood's first – and in my opinion best – adult treatment of the haunted house theme. She was obviously speaking from the heart in it when she said that to a writer everybody else's job is fascinating when compared to his own grinding task. For many of us, writing is the only thing we can do well, we *have* to do it to keep a roof over our heads, and yet we will go to any lengths to put off that moment when we sit down at the desk and make a start.

I think this happens because the only way to do the job properly is to surrender oneself to it completely, to abandon one's existence for a time in favour of the dream-existence of the story. When I'm engrossed in writing a novel the characters in it become more 'real' to me than many in everyday life. What it boils down to is that the writer has to agree to 'die' for a while. Some innermost part of us strenuously objects to the idea of this mini-death, and therefore we can find it very difficult to pick up the pen again.

The above explains why even the keenest amateur, who writes not because he has to but because he *loves* it, will sometimes find himself shying away from the object of his desire. It is up to the individual to work out his own route through or around this problem, but others who have been there before have come up with certain useful tricks.

One is the establishment of routine or habit. Set some kind of daily or weekly production target and do your best to achieve it. Daily is better than weekly because the frequency reinforces habit, but that isn't always practicable for someone who has other employment. You could decide to work a certain number of hours per day or week, but the best way to control your output is with a fixed number of words. It is all too easy to spend a busy hour at the desk doing things like sharpening pencils and cleaning all those grimy marks from the keyboard. You will have *worked*, but in terms of becoming a writer you will have done nothing.

The word target must be tailored to suit you as a unique individual. It should be worth achieving, but not so high that the occasional failure to get there will engender feelings of unworthiness or despair. A thousand words a day is a very popular figure – I suspect because it is such a nice round number – but setting a goal which suits you is easily the most important consideration. I know some successful authors who struggle to produce a thousand words in a week; I know others who can write 8,000 words in one session – a figure I can barely achieve in a day's copy-typing. It is worth remembering that a mere 150 words a day will result in a novel a year.

Another practical method, strange although it may sound, is to *stop* a writing session when you don't really feel like stopping it. Every now and then the writer experiences something like a power surge. The Muse is not only smiling, she is grinning all over her face; enthusiasm is at fever pitch; the fingers are flying over the keyboard and beautiful prose is simply spilling on to the page.

When that happens there is a natural compulsion to keep on and on while the going is good. Make the most of the golden hour, by all means, but it can be highly profitable to stop and withdraw just before all passion has been spent. If you do keep on to the climax (there are times when I wish Freud had never been born) a sense of let-down will often follow, and that will make it more difficult to resume work the next day. Even if you leave off with only one or two sentences in reserve, on the next day traces of the creative high will linger and you will find yourself actually impatient to get back to work.

A variant of this technique is one which may sound trivial in the extreme, but which is useful when no high spots are in view to stimulate productivity. It is actually an exercise in self-deception or confidence trickery. When finishing your day's writing session, compose the final sentence – and put only the first few words of it on the page.

The following evening you may feel lethargic after a solid meal and the television may seem rather tempting. You *know* you should resume writing, but the prospect lacks its usual appeal. At that point you say to yourself, 'I'll just go and finish the last sentence – I can cope with that much – then I'll collapse in the armchair.'

Astonishingly, this simple ruse is often all it takes to get you going again. When *that* sentence has been completed the next one starts coming to mind, and so on . . .

For all we know, Homer and Milton and Shakespeare used similar ploys.

Satisfactory endings

In science fiction it is possible to begin a story at the end. This happens when a really strong or funny line springs to a writer's mind and is recognised as a ready-made conclusion for a short piece of fiction. Work then begins on creating a plausible scenario, a seemingly inevitable way of leading up to the last line.

Science fiction is the best, and almost the only, medium for stories like that. Basically, a fair proportion of them are extended jokes, and have to be kept *very* short. It is up to the author to judge shrewdly the amount of wordage to be expended. I would say that 2,000 is around the upper limit, depending on how much incidental plotting and humour are included, and the quality of the closing line. If you are drawn in that direction and have a weakness for puns, *please* try to ensure that the pay-off pun is a good one.

Literature in general abounds with fictional types who go around making awful puns, and there is a near-conspiracy to make us think that the sheer *badness* of the puns is actually a clever bit of characterisation. We are being asked to believe that, had he so desired, the author could have peppered his stories with excellent puns – but, for the sake of his craft, he has chosen to use bad ones. I always try to avoid being cynical as I wend my way through life, but what do you think?

Starting at the end and working in reverse to the beginning is a good example of back-plotting. It is an interesting clinical experiment to take a well-known phrase or saying and see if, in a minute or so, you can build the inverted pyramid of a short story on it. The following is a micro-story which I have written for this book as an example of what can be done through that kind of conscious motivation.

They're Such Graceful Creatures, Aren't They?

Jane Morton knocked loudly on the front door of the old detached house where her widowed mother lived alone with her pets. There was no reply. An unusual silence reigned within. Suddenly feeling apprehensive, Jane used her key and ventured into the house for the first time in three weeks.

A moment later she came running out, screaming.

That night, even with heavy sedation, she remained ashen-faced, unable to stop reliving every detail of the episode in her mind.

'Why are you so quiet, mother?' she had called as she tapped on the bedroom door.

Why could I not have left it at that? The reproaches yammered incessantly inside her head, with their mess-

age that she would never again be far from the night-
mare. *Why did I have to be flippant?*

And when drugged sleep finally claimed her an hour
later her lips were still silently framing the words she
had uttered in those last few seconds before opening
the bedroom door.

'Has the cat got your tongue?'

And in conclusion . . .

All right, the above is not likely to earn me a Nobel or any
other kind of prize. And it is horror rather than science
fiction – though there is often an affinity between the two.
And I wouldn't be terribly surprised to learn that some
other writer had already used the idea. And cat-lovers may
find it offensive. I don't care about all that. The point I was
making is that a short piece of fiction can be constructed
backwards – constituting another weapon in the armoury of
the beginning writer.

I use the word 'constructed' because a back-plotted story
of this length relies heavily on technical expertise. In the
opening paragraph it was vital to set the scene and acquaint
the reader with the circumstances in a mere handful of
words. Let's re-run the paragraph and this time I will itali-
cise all the words which are there solely for that purpose.

Jane Morton knocked *loudly* on the front door of the
old detached house where her *widowed* mother lived
alone with her *pets*. There was no reply. An *unusual
silence* reigned within. *Suddenly* feeling *apprehensive*,
Jane used her key and *ventured* into the house for the
first time in *three weeks*.

You can see that a hefty amount of literary engineering was going on, but once you understand the method and work hard you can – and *must* – make it unobtrusive. For instance, I could have said that Jane simply 'went into' the house, but the word 'ventured' has connotations of facing the unknown and therefore adds to a sense of unease.

So far in this section I have mainly been talking about the last lines in stories, which were more or less humorous or whimsical or playful in intent, but there is an honourable tradition of totally serious stories finishing with a whiplash in the tail. The Arthur C. Clarke story mentioned earlier – 'Before Eden' – is a prime example.

Another of the grandmaster's offerings was his 1953 short story 'The Nine Billion Names of God'. The thesis was that in Tibet there was a monastery where the monks' lives were dedicated to the belief that the purpose of human existence was to write down, using all permutations of a few letters in their alphabet, the nine billion possible names of God. Once that goal had been achieved the universe would cease to be. The monks had been labouring on their project for centuries, and had not got very far with their quill pens, but now computer technology was at hand. The viewpoint character was an atheistic computer salesman who was congratulating himself on having sold and delivered to the monks a machine capable of printing out the nine billion letter-combinations in a matter of hours.

On his way down the mountain he was concerned to notice – and this is one of the best-known closing lines in all of science fiction – that 'overhead, without any fuss, the stars were going out.'

It goes to show that a short story doesn't have to be like a mallow or a meringue. It can be the literary equivalent of a neutron star – packing a lot of weight into a very small compass. The moral here for the new sf writer is not to fear being ambitious. You might fail if you aim high, but you will never get far by deciding to aim low.

9

GOING TO MARKET

Why do people write? There is a spectrum of answers to the question. At one end of the range you may discover a top politician who finds himself in need of a million or two, and, although he has no interest in words, decides to write a few best-sellers, and actually succeeds in doing so. At the other end is the pure word-lover who is entranced by all the intricate beauties of language, and who wants nothing more than to be left in privacy to explore his own potential.

Between those two extremes there are the vast majority of 'ordinary' writers whose motivations are often complex and may be unfathomable, even to themselves. In some cases it could simply be that a person knows he has something to say – but has nobody to say it *to*. Or, even worse, he has plenty of people around him, but they don't listen because he has the sort of voice which gets drowned out at parties, or because he has a reticent personality, or because his thoughts are much too complicated/radical/esoteric for run-of-the-mill conversations. There can be many other reasons for writing, some of them highly personal and emotive.

In my own case, there was a sprinkling of the above influences, *plus* the fact that my mother derided my youthful yearnings to be an author – and devoted a lot of time to assuring me that I had absolutely no ability and would never be able to sell a word. The desire to prove her wrong was a spur which kept me going when the prospects of getting into print did not look rosy.

What, you may be asking, has that got to do with a how-to-be-a-writer book?

And the answer is: *fear of rejection*.

There is no way of knowing how many people have completed short stories or novels, and then have consigned them to the oblivion of a shoebox in a cupboard. If my personal sampling is statistically valid for the population, the number must be *vast*. It could easily be that some of the best fiction ever produced will never see the light of day. The main reason is that the authors are engaged in what psychologists refer to as a transference. Having put part of themselves into a story, the authors feel that if it is turned down *they* too are being rejected, or in some way being deemed unworthy.

The first thing you have to do, if you want to be a writer, is to put all that behind you. *Please!* I got that attitude knocked out of my head the hard way when I first worked as a reporter for a daily newspaper. The news editor might tell me to write 'ten inches' on a topic; and, if I got carried away and produced twelve column inches, a sub-editor would take a pair of scissors and unceremoniously snip off the redundant two inches of my cherished prose. I soon learned.

It's a somewhat different matter with fiction, of course, but the point remains that if you have worked hard to produce a story you should have equal determination to ensure that others get the opportunity to read it. And do not become a defeatist. In the case of a short story sent to a magazine, the reason for rejection can be that, purely by chance, it has just published a similar story. If you let a year go by the self-same story may be gladly accepted. I have even had the pleasurable experience of having a magazine editor, who had previously rejected a story, writing to me and asking if he could have it back. And I've had the even more pleasurable experience of being able to say, 'Tough luck! You had your chance, but the story has been sold elsewhere.'

Basic presentation

Manuscripts must be in typescript, with double line spacing, on one side only of white A4 paper. You should leave a sensible margin at the top, bottom and sides – the idea being to produce pages which are neither crammed nor unduly sparse. A slim column of words per page looks elegant, but results in your MS being perhaps twice as heavy as necessary. Bear in mind that the people on the receiving end have to transport and read a lot of MSS, and their arms can get as tired as anybody else's.

Editors and agents have to do a great deal of reading, and quite naturally they want to conserve their eyesight – so make sure your typewriter or printer ribbon is fresh and giving a strong, clear impression. In **black**.

The pages should be numbered. Not only should they be numbered – I know how superfluous this sounds – but they should be numbered consecutively and right through to the end. I have seen book-length manuscripts, written by word processor, in which the numbering began afresh at 1 in each chapter, obviously because the author had not found the knack of making his machine think consecutively. It is better to number the pages by hand than to do that.

For your own security reasons, try to imagine the office of a busy editor or agent. The place will be piled high with manuscripts, many of them as yet unread, some of them coming adrift from their covering letters, some of them starting to separate into individual pages as the fasteners begin to feel the strain. What happens if somebody knocks over a table or in some other way causes an avalanche? It could be very difficult indeed to get those thousands of sheets of paper back into their original relationships. There doesn't even have to be a physical accident – in the normal toings and froings of office life piles of paper can be inadvertently mingled and shuffled.

That is why it is worth taking pains to identify your precious work comprehensively. For a start, your covering letter should always quote the name of the work you are submitting. Next, the front page of the MS should state the title, your name, and an estimate of the number of words. It is also helpful if you include the total number of pages. If you are using a pseudonym be sure to add your real name and address. And for complete security, although it means some extra work, it is a good idea to put the title and author's name on *every* page of a manuscript.

It is natural and businesslike to strive to impress an editor with the professional appearance of your MS, but do not fall into the trap of overdoing things. Beginning writers will sometimes go to a lot of trouble and expense to dress a manuscript up in a plushy, massive binding. The theory, conscious or otherwise, is that if the MS in its raw state already looks and feels like a published work the editor will subliminally be coaxed to look on it with approval.

Nice try, but things don't work out that way. Editors and agents are not so easily influenced. In fact, the elaborate bindings can be counter-productive. Keep in mind the picture of these people as practical, hard-pressed human beings who have to be as effective as possible in order to succeed. They have to do a *lot* of reading, and they school themselves to do it anywhere under any conditions.

At the end of the office day, a busy editor may look at a thick manuscript and say, 'I could read half of that tomorrow morning on the train.' His briefcase is already bulging, so what does he do? He splits the MS in two, and is not at all impressed by the fancy binding which only makes the task more difficult. (On a related point, if you use a word processor do not try to improve the acceptability of your manuscript by justifying the right-hand margins. Editors positively dislike that because it can confuse the computers used by their printing contractors, thus leading to strange typographical effects and expensive extra work.)

The best plan is to use a binding which is adequate but plain and adaptable. Thin A4 card is fine for front and back, and those two-pronged metal fasteners are usually all that is needed to keep the lot together.

How long will you be?

One could be forgiven for assuming that, among all the uncertainties and shifting tides of creative writing, there will be one trustworthy invariant – namely, the number of words in a story. What could be simpler than reckoning how many words there are in a manuscript?

Hah!

At this point human nature raises its homely head again, and the situation is complicated by some technical considerations. Established authors, selling to magazines which have a fixed word rate, are subject to a malady of perception which often leads them to over-estimate the number of words they are actually turning in. The disease used to be quite endemic in the early days of vernacular publishing when the custom was to pay hack writers by the line. They became adept at producing long chains of dialogue in which the participants could only communicate in single words, rather like the exclamation which preceded this paragraph.

On the other hand, new writers – anxious to get a toe in

the door by giving excellent value for money – sometimes tend to diminish their work. I have seen amateur MSS containing easily 8,000 words which the author has been content to retail at a stated 5,000.

The word processor is rapidly supplanting the typewriter, and one might think that signals the end of the problem. My modest machine will quickly tell me the exact number of words in any piece of work – but all authors know very well that the *gaps* have to be taken into consideration as well. There has never been a manuscript, or publication, in which every line was packed from edge to edge with the maximum number of typographical characters.

The most reasonable scheme for estimating word length is to mark off, say, twenty typical lines in your manuscript. The sample should include a paragraph indentation or two, and perhaps a piece of dialogue – whatever you judge representative of your general output. Count the exact number of words in it and divide by twenty, thus reaching a fair approximation of the number of words per line. Multiply that figure by how many lines you always put on a page and you will have an estimate of the number of words per page that no reasonably minded editor could disagree with. From there it is easy to go on and calculate the total 'true' word-length of your manuscript, and thus its market value.

Almost into the mailbox

The last thing to be done before packaging a manuscript for the post is to write the famous 'covering letter'.

Editors and agents alike ask just one thing of you in this respect – keep the letter short and businesslike. It is usually enough to say something like: 'Dear . . . , I am enclosing a short story/novelette/novel entitled . . . which I hope you will consider good enough for publication. I also enclose return postage. Yours sincerely.'

Resist all temptation to try any kind of selling. It is a pure waste of time to go into what prompted you to write the story, the difficulties encountered on the way, the enthusiastic reactions of your friends and family, the weak spots in the narrative which are compensated for by the grand finale . . . The hard facts are that your brain-child has to stand on its own two feet, completely unaided, once you send it out into the world. You can't hover around it like a guardian angel and protect it. Everything that has to be said should be said in the work itself – otherwise you have failed to discharge your responsibilities as an author.

The literary agent

This is a subject which generates a lot of discussion in writing circles, especially among newcomers. At one pole there is the person who says, 'Why should I pay ten per cent, or even fifteen per cent, of my earnings to a guy who just forwards my stuff to a publisher?' At the other pole is the person whose complaint is, 'I'm never going to get published without the help of an agent, but no agent will take me on because I've never been published.'

When someone asks me if I regard a literary agent as a necessity, my answer is an emphatic *yes*. I know one or two authors who are sufficiently experienced, business-minded and energetic to be able to represent themselves – but they are a great rarity. For the rest of us, it makes more sense to concentrate on the writing and leave it to an expert to deal with business matters.

However, a lot depends on the writer's individual circumstances, and what he wants to get out of writing. Throughout this book I have dealt with short fiction as much as with the novel. The reason was twofold: (a) the short-story form is naturally attractive to the new writer, especially when there is a full-time job to be coped with; (b) there is a market for sf short stories. It's not as large as it used to be, but it is still there and shows no signs of going away.

This is where we have to start talking about money. The sad fact about sf short stories is that it is impossible to earn a living from them. Nobody regrets that more than I do – I *love* writing short stories – but there it is. Immediately, therefore, in purely monetary terms, and leaving artistic inclinations aside, beginning writers are divided into two camps.

The first is made up of those who mainly want a hobby or sideline which will yield a nice bit of extra pocket money. In that case, they are free to devote as much time as they choose to the writing of short stories. The second camp is comprised of those who have set their sights on making money in largish chunks, and perhaps becoming full-time authors. They *must* give due priority to the novel.

The relevance of the above to the subject of agents is that, in general, it is not really worth an agency's time and trouble to sell a short story. Eleanor Wood, who heads the Spectrum Agency in New York, said to me, 'Magazines and anthologies usually operate on a fixed word rate, so the agent has no room to do any manoeuvring on the client's behalf. And by the time we do all the processing our costs usually exceed the profit. When I handle a short story for a client it is almost doing a favour.'

The message is that, if you are going to concentrate on short fiction, agents will have no part to play in your life. You should proceed by doing your own survey of the market and making your own submissions.

Market research is a serious obligation, not something to be taken lightly. As I said in an earlier chapter, it is not a good idea to write a story and then try to think of a place to sell it. I have published about eighty short stories, and in nearly all of them knew in advance – *during the writing* – which magazines they would appear in. I made it my business not only to read but to *study* the magazines. I learned the names of the editors to help me familiarise myself with them as people. I almost memorised their editorials. Not only did I know what they were currently buying – I could make a good guess at what they would be buying in the following year. I have sold 100 per cent of my literary output.

The first person singular pronoun appears a lot in the above paragraph, I have to admit, but it is an advertisement not for me – but for the *method*. The surest way to success is to be informed, to be on top of things, to know your way around. Thanks to modern communications you can be well informed, no matter where you live. The sources quoted in the appendix [4] will link you to an international information network.

The novel approach

Now we come to the business of selling novels. This is where the literary agent becomes pre-eminent. The beginning writer *can* market a novel by himself, my advice being to use much the same approach as described above for short stories. Find out what publishers there are and read a few novels from their lists so that you won't waste time by submitting books which are not compatible with their house style, etc.

An immediate difficulty is that a novel arriving at a publisher's office from an unknown writer is likely to be put into the 'slushpile' until somebody has time to look at it. In a busy office that can be a long time indeed. When a book arrives by way of an agent, the editor is pre-informed that it has been read and approved of by at least one other knowledgeable person. He is then inclined to look at it sooner and to give it more serious consideration.

Here are some other points which more than justify the existence of agents. They, necessarily, know the market very well and can guide MSS in the right direction. They have personal influence with editors and can use it on their clients' behalf in all kinds of issues. Not having to concern themselves about personal modesty – which would limit an author's sales pitch – they can beat the big drum on behalf of a book and promote a better deal. They are expert in interpreting and protecting the author's contractual rights, and thus can maximise his earnings. They have contacts with agents and publishers in other parts of the world which facilitate foreign sales. (Since the terminal corrosion of the Iron Curtain this has become an increasingly important factor in the financial outlook of the working author.)

An agent speaks

Pamela Buckmaster heads the Carnell Literary Agency, the only one in the UK to specialise in science fiction and fantasy. As beginning writers have only the vaguest idea of what to expect in dealings with agents, I decided to put some of their most common questions directly to her . . .

What is the real function of an agent?

'In a nutshell, it is to be on the author's side – a good friend and adviser. Generally speaking, a publisher is concerned with deciding whether or not a book will be a commercial success, and if it will fit into his list. An agent will take a much broader view, and will ponder on different questions. Is there talent here? Is there potential to develop into a major writer? Are there any publishers who will want to take on this writer and invest in their development?'

What does an agent actually do to earn commission?

'The big advantage in having an agent is that the agent has no conflict of interests. The writer and the writer's career must come first. But, as a corollary to that, the publisher must also get a fair deal – writers depend on the existence of healthy, successful publishers. Writers often build up good personal relationships with their editors, but if there is no intermediary to handle the business side the relationship can be put at risk.'

Do you mean they can fall out over a payment?

'Yes, but it could be more serious than that. If there is a personal involvement, the writer can be hindered from moving on to another publisher when it is necessary for the advancement of his or her career. It is then invaluable to have an agent to act as a buffer. In the early days a writer may lean heavily on an editor, and without the backing of an agent may find it very difficult to make a stand.'

It sounds as though you encourage writers to be ruthless and stubborn . . .

'No. Resolute and reasonable would be more like it. Writers

can have their faults, too. One who is unwittingly damaging his own prospects by being unreasonable and stubborn will need sound professional advice, someone to smooth the troubled waters.'

Does an agent advise on the actual writing?

'My own editorial help is strictly confined to analysing the kind of reading experience the writer is aiming for, and giving feedback on what is actually occurring for the reader. There is often a huge gap between the effect the writer thinks the words are having, and what the words on the page are actually doing. I act as a sounding board, thus setting the stage for writers to develop their potential. This is a personal view, but it seems to me that agents, or editors, who do heavy editing for writers are not in the long run doing them a service. Writers learn by rewriting their own work where necessary and getting it right by themselves.'

Is it necessary, or even desirable, for the new writer to submit an entire novel?

'No. It is often better for all concerned if the author sends in two sample chapters and a good synopsis. That is enough to enable an experienced agent to assess the potential of a story.'

How does the new writer actually set about the business of getting an agent?

'The addresses of all the agencies can be obtained from *The Writers' and Artists' Yearbook*, and similar sources. An agency may claim that its list is full, but these things are flexible – no agency is going to turn away someone they think has talent and potential. The best way to get an agent is to make sure that your two sample chapters are unputdownable. In the end, it is all up to the writer.

What if an agent asks for a reading fee?

'There is nothing wrong with that in principle. I don't do it myself, because by the time I've read a submission, and weighed up its prospects, and written as helpful a letter as possible, *and* parcelled the whole thing up again and mailed it back, several hours of my time have been invested. A realistic charge for that would probably stun the hopeful writer.'

And in summation?

'A successful writer's career can span many years and a large number of books. The agent will look after the business side of things; market subsidiary and foreign rights vigorously; keep sight of the whole of an author's *oeuvre* with the objective of exploiting successes and retrieving disasters. It is a very demanding job. We are not magicians – but we do our best.'

The financial rewards

It would be possible to write a chapter on this subject alone. The range of payments is so great, however, and the possible contractual variations so numerous and bewildering, that a lengthy discussion of the matter would be out of place in a book about how to *start* writing science fiction. There is a labyrinth of facts and figures – made more fearsome by the way in which they shift from month to month, prey to a dozen conflicting influences. That, in my opinion, is one of the main reasons for working through an agent.

Nevertheless, the beginning writer is entitled to *some* idea of what to expect.

Let's look at short stories first. As I said earlier, it is impossible to live by writing short fiction. You would be a miracle-worker if you could write one good 5,000-word short story every week. And even if you could do it you wouldn't be able to sell them all – because the market could not absorb that quantity. For those you did manage to sell you would be paid in the region of £30 per thousand words in this country, and perhaps up to £50 for sales to American magazines.

It doesn't take Wall Street training to appreciate that you would be earning less than anybody in the most menial job imaginable. Occasionally a short story can 'click' with a major glossy, such as *Omni* or *Playboy*, and bring in $2,000 or so, but the competition is so fierce that such markets cannot play a part in everyday economics. I would say that the money is not the main thing for the short-story writer. The real reward comes from loving what you are doing in your free time – and if, on the way, you pick up enough cash to buy a new video machine or a foreign holiday, so much the better.

When we come to novels, we are really venturing into the financial wonderland. I know people who have been paid as little as £30 for a novel – and I know others who have been paid more than a million. Between those extremes you find the majority of writers who either (a) enjoy a profitable hobby, (b) make a reasonable living, or (c) do very nicely for themselves.

In this country an advance in the region of £1,000 from a hardback publisher is quite common for a first science-fiction novel, though it could be several times that if the publisher has a lot of confidence. The advance is based on the number of copies the publisher believes he is sure to sell. If the advance is 'earned out', and actual sales figures begin to exceed the projection, the author can then expect twice-yearly royalty cheques. These, if they come, can be quite small – because the publisher's extrapolation was accurate – but the author's income can be further boosted by the sale of paperback rights and by overseas sales. A USA sale, for instance, will usually bring rather more than the UK figure.

I have deliberately adopted a sober tone in the above paragraph because it is important for the new writer to be realistic in his expectations. On the other hand, writing is a weird, wonderful and quite unpredictable profession – and quite a few people have become millionaires through writing science fiction. If you have, or can develop, the magic touch, there is almost no limit to what you may achieve.

Writing science fiction can be almost a science-fictional experience in itself.

Go to it!

APPENDIX

1. Anthologies

Adventures in Time & Space (1946), Raymond J.
  Healey and J. Francis McComas
Dangerous Visions (1968), Harlan Ellison
Again Dangerous Visions (1972), Harlan Ellison
A Science Fiction Argosy (1972), Damon Knight
The Best Science-Fiction Stories (1977), M. Stapleton
The Arbor House Treasury of Modern Science Fiction
  (1980), Robert Silverberg and Martin H.
  Greenberg.
Various annuals – *Year's Best* etc.

2. Reference books

New Maps of Hell (1961), Kingsley Amis
The Encyclopedia of Science Fiction (1979),
  P. Nicholls
The Trillion Year Spree (1986), Brian Aldiss and
  David Wingrove
Science Fiction – The 100 Best Novels (1985), David
  Pringle

3. Mail Order SF Bookshops

Andromeda Bookshop, 84 Suffolk Street,
    Birmingham B1 1TA
Fantast (Medway) Limited, PO Box 23, Upwell,
    Wisbech, Cambs. PE14 9BU

4. Up-to-the-minute Information Sources

British Science Fiction Association (membership
    enquiries): Joanne Raine, 29 Thornville Road,
    Hartlepool, Cleveland TS26 8EW

The Science Fiction Foundation, Polytechnic of East
    London, Longbridge Road, Dagenham RM8 2AS

5. Magazines

Interzone Science Fiction and Fantasy, 217 Preston
    Drove, Brighton BN1 6FL (for current fiction
    and news)